Globalisation

Editor: Danielle Lobban

Volume 416

independence
educational publishers

First published by Independence Educational Publishers

The Studio, High Green

Great Shelford

Cambridge CB22 5EG

England

© Independence 2023

ISBN-13: 978 1 86168 876 7

Printed in Great Britain

Zenith Print Group

Acknowledgements

The publisher is grateful for permission to reproduce the material in this book. While every care has been taken to trace and acknowledge copyright, the publisher tenders its apology for any accidental infringement or where copyright has proved untraceable. The publisher would be pleased to come to a suitable arrangement in any such case with the rightful owner.

The material reproduced in **issues** books is provided as an educational resource only. The views, opinions and information contained within reprinted material in **issues** books do not necessarily represent those of Independence Educational Publishers and its employees.

Images

Cover image courtesy of iStock. All other images courtesy of Freepik, Pixabay and Unsplash,

Additional acknowledgements

With thanks to the Independence team: Shelley Baldry, Tracy Biram, Klaudia Sommer and Jackie Staines.

Danielle Lobban

Cambridge, January 2023

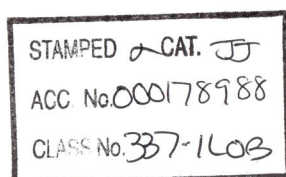

Contents

Chapter 1: What is Globalisation?

Chapter 2: A Shrinking World?

Introduction

Globalisation is Volume 416 in the **issues** series. The aim of the series is to offer current, diverse information about important issues in our world, from a UK perspective.

About Globalisation

Is the world really shrinking? Globalisation means that our world is ever-connected, while some think it is in decline, others think it will continue to grow, or change shape. This book explores the effects of globalisation on different areas of our lives, from economic to cultural and beyond.

Our sources

Titles in the **issues** series are designed to function as educational resource books, providing a balanced overview of a specific subject.

The information in our books is comprised of facts, articles and opinions from many different sources, including:

- Newspaper reports and opinion pieces
- Website factsheets
- Magazine and journal articles
- Statistics and surveys
- Government reports
- Literature from special interest groups.

A note on critical evaluation

Because the information reprinted here is from a number of different sources, readers should bear in mind the origin of the text and whether the source is likely to have a particular bias when presenting information (or when conducting their research). It is hoped that, as you read about the many aspects of the issues explored in this book, you will critically evaluate the information presented.

It is important that you decide whether you are being presented with facts or opinions. Does the writer give a biased or unbiased report? If an opinion is being expressed, do you agree with the writer? Is there potential bias to the 'facts' or statistics behind an article?

Activities

Throughout this book, you will find a selection of assignments and activities designed to help you engage with the articles you have been reading and to explore your own opinions. Some tasks will take longer than others and there is a mixture of design, writing and research-based activities that you can complete alone or in a group.

Further research

At the end of each article we have listed its source and a website that you can visit if you would like to conduct your own research. Please remember to critically evaluate any sources that you consult and consider whether the information you are viewing is accurate and unbiased.

Issues Online

The **issues** series of books is complimented by our online resource, issuesonline.co.uk

On the Issues Online website you will find a wealth of information, covering over 70 topics, to support the PSHE and RSE curriculum.

Why Issues Online?

Researching a topic? Issues Online is the best place to start for...

Librarians

Issues Online is an essential tool for librarians: feel confident you are signposting safe, reliable, user-friendly online resources to students and teaching staff alike. We provide multi-user concurrent access, so no waiting around for another student to finish with a resource. Issues Online also provides FREE downloadable posters for your shelf/wall/table displays.

Teachers

Issues Online is an ideal resource for lesson planning, inspiring lively debate in class and setting lessons and homework tasks.

Our accessible, engaging content helps deepen student's knowledge, promotes critical thinking and develops independent learning skills.

Issues Online saves precious preparation time. We wade through the wealth of material on the internet to filter the best quality, most relevant and up-to-date information you need to start exploring a topic.

Our carefully selected, balanced content presents an overview and insight into each topic from a variety of sources and viewpoints.

Students

Issues Online is designed to support your studies in a broad range of topics, particularly social issues relevant to young people today.

Thousands of articles, statistics and infographs instantly available to help you with research and assignments.

With 24/7 access using the powerful Algolia search system, you can find relevant information quickly, easily and safely anytime from your laptop, tablet or smartphone, in class or at home.

Visit issuesonline.co.uk to find out more!

issues online
resources for schools, colleges & libraries

What is Globalisation?

What is globalisation?

Globalisation is a word that gets thrown around a lot, often as part of vague and slightly suspect declarations about progress by politicians and CEOs alike (do you think they're trying to sell us something…?), but what this really means for us on a day to day level can get lost in the aspirational – some might say, delusional – rhetoric.

So, to call a spade a spade, here is globalisation laid bare: it is a juggernaut economic system brought about by governments' international deregulation of trade and finance. This lack of restrictions has enabled businesses and banks to expand and function globally, unhindered by borders – or even, say, laws – and resulted in a single world market; one controlled by transnational corporations rather than by local economies and communities, who nonetheless happen to provide its labour force. Still buying It?

This economy is the unstable and unsustainable culmination of a long-standing ideal held in western Europe for the past 500 years, later encapsulated by the American Dream during the 20th Century. Dream, however, being the operative word, as its lofty aims for an ever bigger, better, brighter future (i.e., economic abundance for all) cannot abide by our planet's reality and all the unshakeable limitations which are inherent to life on Earth.

Instead, globalisation tries to bend both people and planet to the will of the market – and the overall outcome is far from prosperous. In this modern age of convenience and astronomical profits, we're facing the inconvenient and astronomical disasters of economic collapse, the climate emergency, mass extinction, eroding democracy, increasing violence and fundamentalism, a soaring mental health crisis, and pandemics.

Globalisation tries to bend both people and planet to the will of the market – and the overall outcome is far from prosperous

Shouldn't we have 'made it' to wherever we're supposed to be going by now? Nope. Because, despite evident disfunction (listed above), that's not the point. Quite the opposite. Growth is the only logic of globalisation – all else be quite literally damned.

It actually – illogically – all stems from outdated attitudes that don't make sense in the world today (not that they were ever morally 'sound'). For centuries, Europeans remained bent on conquering and colonising abroad. They dismantled self-reliant communities and enslaved populations to enrich their own. These days, imperialism remains visible in the dressed-up western model of outsourcing cheap labour to the Global South; in foreign resource extraction; as well as in vast aid packages and loans, which shackle LEDCs (less economically developed countries) with immense debt to the wealthy, developed world.

And as poorer nations fall further into resultant poverty, companies are still better able to exploit them, growing ever-richer; able to demand ever-more deregulation from their desperate governments, causing ever-more destruction to people and ecosystems – globally.

The story

On its polished surface, globalisation is the worldwide exchange of cultures and ideas, of education and opportunities, products and services; an opening up of the planet's places and resources and wealth for all to access. Sounds good. That's the theory anyway – one propped up by corporate-funded think tanks and dispensed far-and-wide in advertising campaigns.

So why then, rather than expanding connection, has globalisation actually managed to diminish it in terms of practical, everyday life? CEOs and workers are as far-removed from each other as chalk and cheese; or moreover as producers from consumers; as food and farming; as people from the land.

What's more, making consumer and investment choices that align with our individual values is near impossible in today's society: the market just isn't set up for it. In fact, we are basically set up around the market.

The reality

In reality, globalisation has primarily become – like most things these days – an economic affair, with GDP taking precedence over all else, far surmounting well-being on the political agenda. Because in a globalised world, all of society is subject to one increasingly singular growth imperative – and one (white-majority western) monoculture too. Conformity is the only option, but no guarantee of individual prosperity, especially for indigenous groups or those in the debt ridden Global South.

Our livelihoods and culture are determined by the needs of the growing economy, rather than the reverse, which you'd think would be a given. This means that daily life is based more in artificial projections than any mutual communion with the natural world around us. Globalisation has ultimately cost us our connection with our local environment, and as we 'grow', we merely grow this distance, losing touch with the needs of our ecosystem; indeed, counteracting them.

In fact, one of the central tenets of this now-global dream, that our children would have it better (i.e., more) than us, has now been lost along the way. We've changed our outlook entirely amidst the onwards motion: it's commonly accepted that future generations have it far worse than ever as a result of our ongoing activities today. And yet we continue, business as usual, while apathy gradually replaces hope in public consciousness.

We need to see past the figures and look to our own local communities; to measure prosperity on an authentic, human scale; on levels of self-reliance and localised sustainability rather than the amount of access we may currently have to global resources – a mismatch characteristic to the modern, globalised west. A better, more truly prosperous world – that's for both people and planet, not just 'on the page' in terms of GDP – requires that the concept of progress be equally accountable to an area's poverty levels, not profits alone, which at best only reach a bare few whilst depriving the majority.

The above information is reprinted with kind permission from EcoResolution.
© 2022 EcoResolution

www.ecoresolution.earth

What caused globalisation?

By Tejvan Pettinger

Globalisation is not a new phenomenon. The world economy has become increasingly interdependent for a long time. However, in recent decades the process of globalisation has accelerated; this is due to a variety of factors, but important ones include improved trade, increased labour and capital mobility and improved technology.

Main reasons that have caused globalisation

1. Improved transport, making global travel easier. For example, there has been a rapid growth in air travel, enabling greater movement of people and goods across the globe.

2. Containerisation. From 1970, there was a rapid adoption of the steel transport container. This reduced the costs of inter-modal transport, making trade cheaper and more efficient.

3. Improved technology which makes it easier to communicate and share information around the world. (E.g. the internet, for example, to work on improvements on a website, I will go to a global online community. There, people from any country can bid for the right to provide a service. It means that I can often find people to do a job relatively cheaply because labour costs are relatively lower in the Indian sub-continent.)

4. Growth of multinational companies with a global presence in many different economies.

5. Growth of global trading blocks which have reduced national barriers. (e.g. European Union, NAFTA, ASEAN)

6. Reduced tariff barriers which encourage global trade. Often this has occurred through the support of the WTO.

7. Firms exploiting gains from economies of scale to gain increased specialisation. This is an essential feature of new trade theory.

Main causes of globalisation

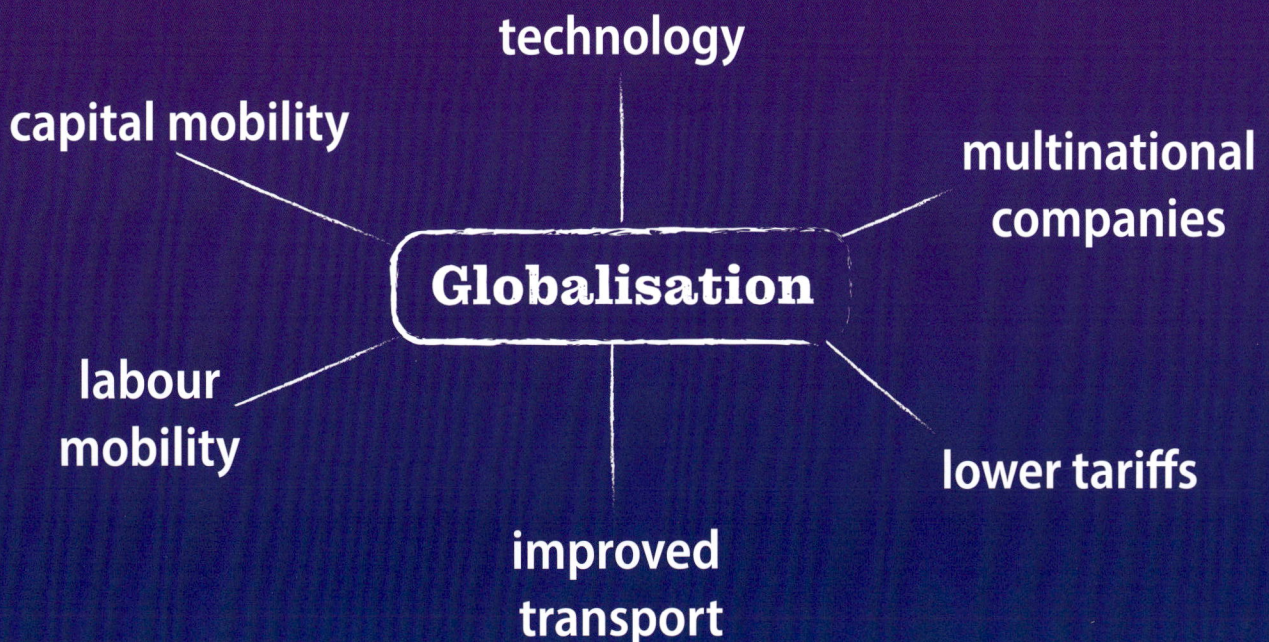

technology

capital mobility

multinational companies

Globalisation

labour mobility

lower tariffs

improved transport

Source: www.economicshelp.org

Average global tariff %

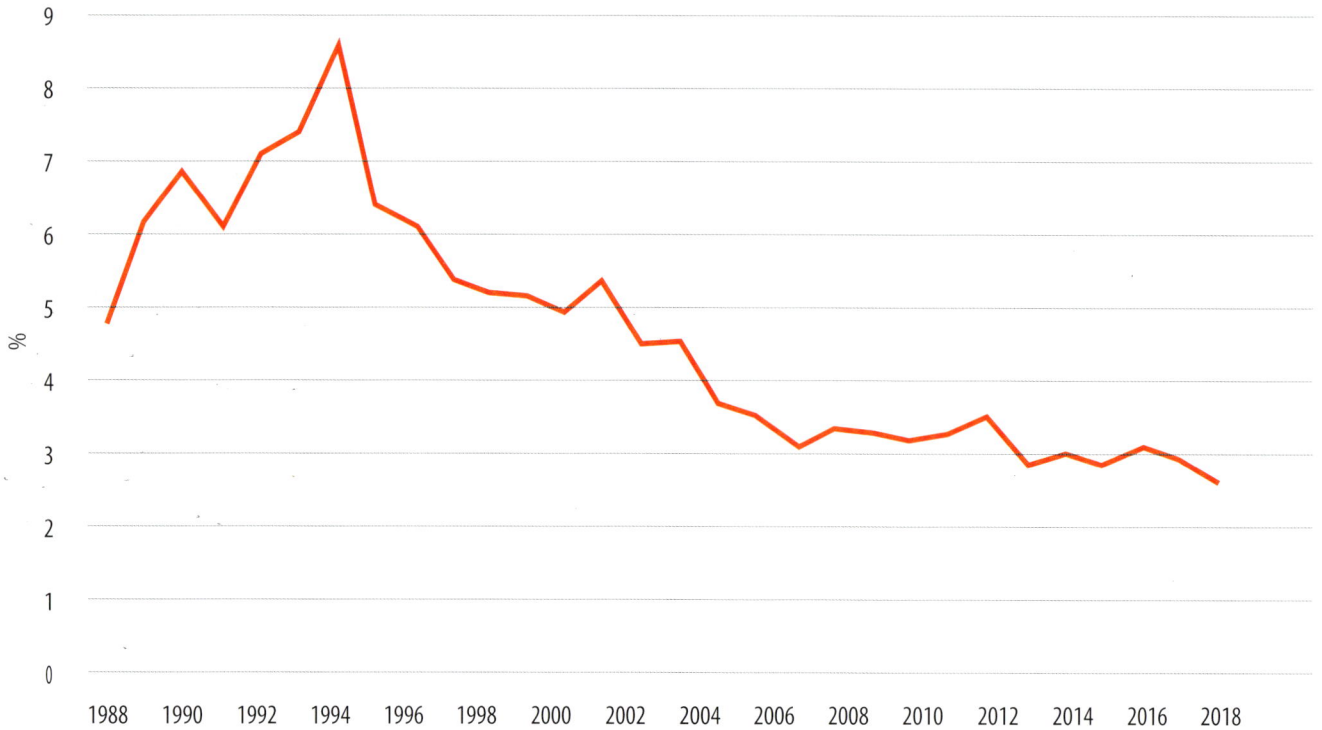

Source: World Bank - Tariff Rate, applied, weighted mean, all products % - TM.TAX.MRCH.WM.AR.ZS

8. Growth of global media.
9. Global trade cycle. Economic growth is global in nature. This means countries are increasingly interconnected. (E.g. recession in one country affects global trade and invariably causes an economic downturn in major trading partners.)
10. Financial system increasingly global in nature. When US banks suffered losses due to the sub-prime mortgage

World exports as % GDP

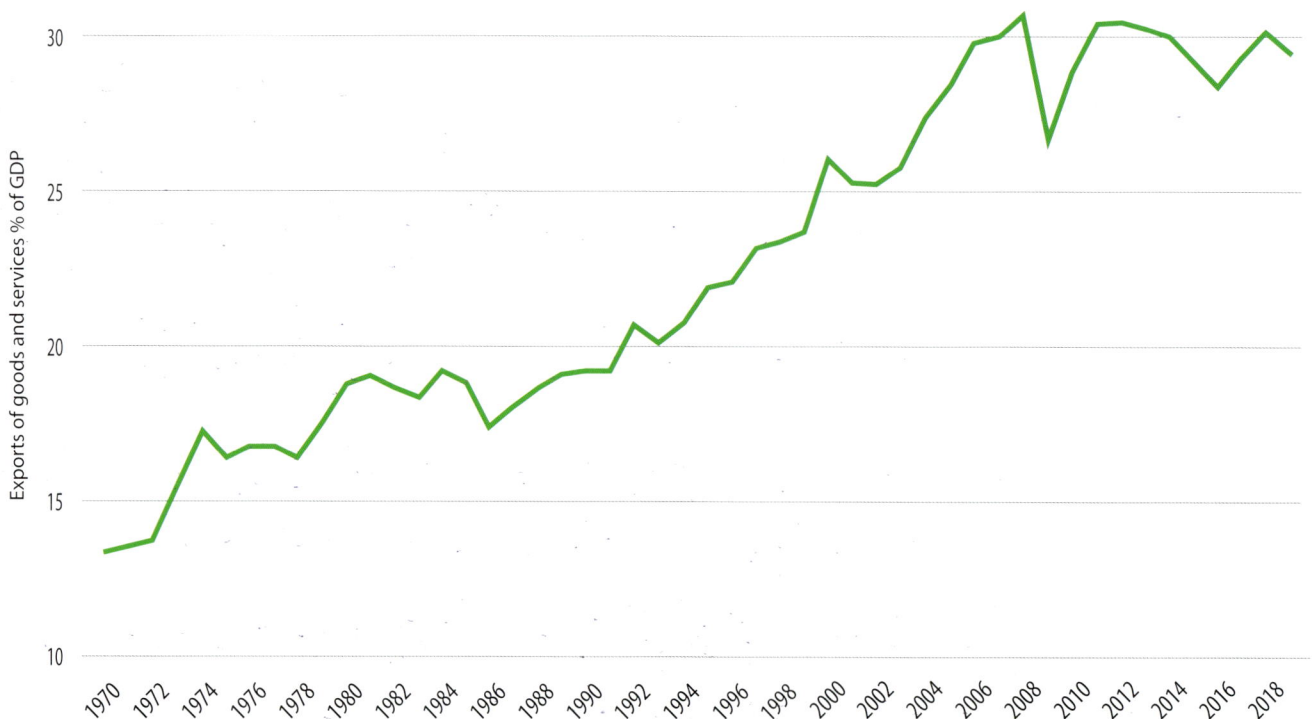

Source: World Bank - ID: NE.EXPGNFS.ZS - accessed 4 Sept 2021

World exports of goods and services

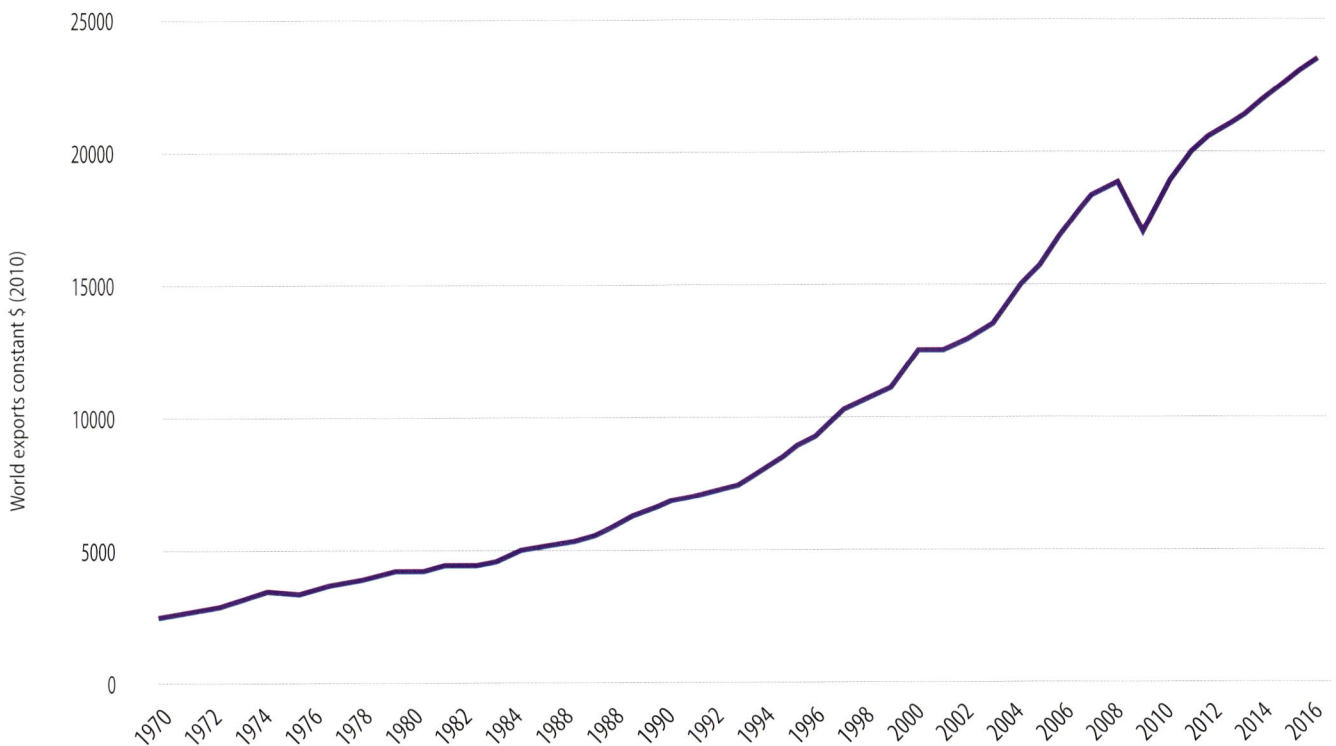

World exports constant $ (2010)

Source: World Bank - NE.EXPGNFS.KD

crisis, it affected all major banks in other countries who had bought financial derivatives from US banks and mortgage companies.

11. Improved mobility of capital. In the past few decades, there has been a general reduction in capital barriers, making it easier for capital to flow between different economies. This has increased the ability for firms to receive finance. It has also increased the global interconnectedness of global financial markets.

12. Increased mobility of labour. People are more willing to move between different countries in search for work. Global trade remittances now play a large role in transfers from developed countries to developing countries.

13. Internet. This enables firms to communicate on a global level, this may overcome managerial diseconomies of scale. The firm may be able to get cheaper supplies by dealing with a wider choice of firms. Consumers are also able to order more goods online, e.g. Dell Computers takes orders online and can meet customer specifications.

Evaluation of globalisation

- It is hard to precisely define globalisation, there are different interpretations of what we actually mean, therefore, there are different factors that explain it.

- Improved technology is undoubtedly very influential in helping globalisation; without technologies such as the internet and global communication, it would not have been possible to witness the increased interdependence of companies and countries.

- Increased free trade is important. However, there are various trade barriers still in existence, and this has not stopped the growth of globalisation.

- Could there be a backlash against globalisation as people look for local alternatives to multinational products? I think this is unlikely as people prefer the security of buying established brand names but 'buy local' has increasing popularity amongst some people.

Is globalisation irreversible?

Probably not. The history of humanity is one of globalisation. The factors that have been behind globalisation in the past, are likely to continue. However, it is possible to change certain factors. For example, it is possible for countries to place tariff barriers and restrict immigration. But, this is only a partial block to the process of globalisation. In terms of growth of trade as % of world GDP, it may be we have reached a plateau at just under 30% of GDP.

Exports are increasingly important to the world economy.

6 April 2021

A brief history of globalisation

By Peter Vanham, Deputy Head of Media, World Economic Forum Geneva

When Chinese e-commerce giant Alibaba in 2018 announced it had chosen the ancient city of Xi'an as the site for its new regional headquarters, the symbolic value wasn't lost on the company: it had brought globalisation to its ancient birthplace, the start of the old Silk Road. It named its new offices aptly: 'Silk Road Headquarters'. The city where globalisation had started more than 2,000 years ago would also have a stake in globalisation's future.

Alibaba shouldn't be alone in looking back. As we are entering a new, digital-driven era of globalisation – we call it 'Globalisation 4.0' – it is worthwhile that we do the same. When did globalisation start? What were its major phases? And where is it headed tomorrow?

So, when did international trade start and how did it lead to globalisation?

Silk roads (1st century BC-5th century AD, and 13th-14th centuries AD)

People have been trading goods for almost as long as they've been around. But as of the 1st century BC, a remarkable phenomenon occurred. For the first time in history, luxury products from China started to appear on the other edge of the Eurasian continent – in Rome. They got there after being hauled for thousands of miles along the Silk Road. Trade had stopped being a local or regional affair and started to become global.

That is not to say globalisation had started in earnest. Silk was mostly a luxury good, and so were the spices that were added to the intercontinental trade between Asia and Europe. As a percentage of the total economy, the value of these exports was tiny, and many middlemen were involved to get the goods to their destination. But global trade links were established, and for those involved, it was a goldmine. From purchase price to final sales price, the multiple went in the dozens. The Silk Road could prosper in part because two great empires dominated much of the route. If trade was interrupted, it was most often because of blockades by local enemies of Rome or China. If the Silk Road eventually closed, as it did after several centuries, the fall of the empires had everything to do with it. And when it reopened in Marco Polo's late medieval time, it was because of the rise of a new hegemonic empire: the Mongols. It is a pattern we'll see throughout the history of trade: it thrives when nations protect it, it falls when they don't.

Globalisation era	Age of Discovery 15th – 18th century	Globalisation 1.0 19th century - 1914	Globalisation 2.0 1945 - 1989	Globalisation 3.0 1989-2008	Globalisation 4.0
Leading exports	Raw materials/ basic goods	Textiles/ industrial goods	Factories	Global supply chain	Digital goods/ services
Leading nations	Spain, Portugal, UK, Netherlands	UK	USA, China	USA	USA, China
Exports as % world GDP	<5%	6 - 14%	5 - 15%	15 - >20%	?
Enabling era	Scientific Revolution 15th - 17th century	1st Industrial Revolution 1780s - mid 19th century	2nd Industrial Revolution 1870s - 1910s	3rd Industrial Revolution 1960s - 1990s	4th Industrial Revolution 2000s - 2010s
Enabling innovations	(sailing ship, compass)	(locomotive, steamship)	(truck, aeroplane)	(computer, www)	(cloud, wireless)
Characterising GDP trend	Europe	Britain	World	United States	China

Source: World Economic Forum

Spice routes (7th-15th centuries)

The next chapter in trade happened thanks to Islamic merchants. As the new religion spread in all directions from its Arabian heartland in the 7th century, so did trade. The founder of Islam, the prophet Mohammed, was famously a merchant, as was his wife Khadija. Trade was thus in the DNA of the new religion and its followers, and that showed. By the early 9th century, Muslim traders already dominated Mediterranean and Indian Ocean trade; afterwards, they could be found as far east as Indonesia, which over time became a Muslim-majority country, and as far west as Moorish Spain.

The main focus of Islamic trade in those Middle Ages were spices. Unlike silk, spices were traded mainly by sea since ancient times. But by the medieval era they had become the true focus of international trade. Chief among them were the cloves, nutmeg and mace from the fabled Spice islands – the Maluku islands in Indonesia. They were extremely expensive and in high demand, also in Europe. But as with silk, they remained a luxury product, and trade remained relatively low volume. Globalisation still didn't take off, but the original Belt (sea route) and Road (Silk Road) of trade between East and West did now exist.

Age of Discovery (15th-18th centuries)

Truly global trade kicked off in the Age of Discovery. It was in this era, from the end of the 15th century onwards, that European explorers connected East and West – and accidentally discovered the Americas. Aided by the discoveries of the so-called 'Scientific Revolution' in the fields of astronomy, mechanics, physics and shipping, the Portuguese, Spanish and later the Dutch and the English first 'discovered', then subjugated, and finally integrated new lands in their economies.

The Age of Discovery rocked the world. The most (in)famous 'discovery' is that of America by Columbus, which all but ended pre-Colombian civilizations. But the most consequential exploration was the circumnavigation by Magellan: it opened the door to the Spice islands, cutting out Arab and Italian middlemen. While trade once again remained small compared to total GDP, it certainly altered people's lives. Potatoes, tomatoes, coffee and chocolate were introduced in Europe, and the price of spices fell steeply.

Major economies dropped tariff rates and kept them low

Average applied tariff rates (1988-2020)

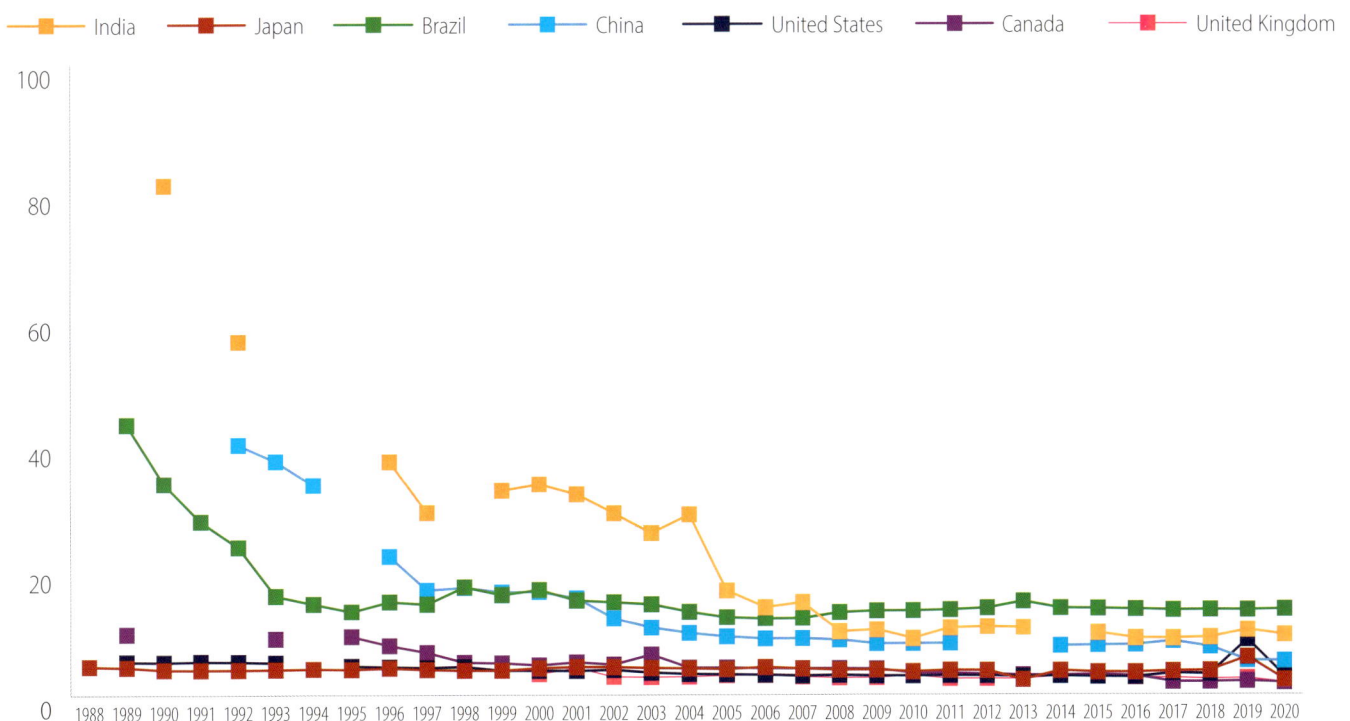

Note: Shows world's ten largest economies, 2020. Rates are weighted by trade value.
Source: World Bank Data Bank

Trade grew to a third of the US economy and over half of the world's economy

World and US trade as a percent of GDP (1960-2016)

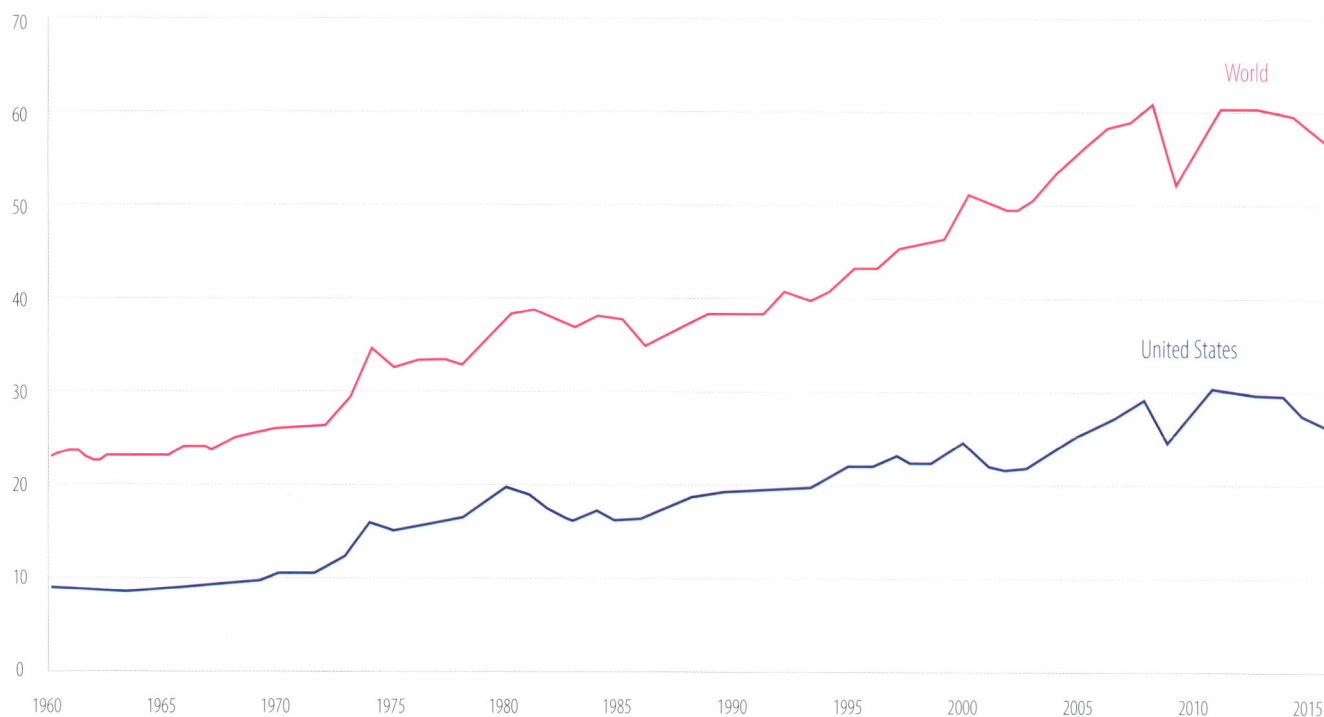

Source: World Bank: World Bank DataBank and International Debt Statistics, International Monetary Fund: International Financial Statistics and Balance if Payments databases; GDP estimates from World Bank and Organization for Economic Cooperation and Development

Yet economists today still don't truly regard this era as one of true globalisation. Trade certainly started to become global, and it had even been the main reason for starting the Age of Discovery. But the resulting global economy was still very much siloed and lopsided. The European empires set up global supply chains, but mostly with those colonies they owned. Moreover, their colonial model was chiefly one of exploitation, including the shameful legacy of the slave trade. The empires thus created both a mercantilist and a colonial economy, but not a truly globalized one.

First wave of globalisation (19th century-1914)

This started to change with the first wave of globalisation, which roughly occurred over the century ending in 1914. By the end of the 18th century, Great Britain had started to dominate the world both geographically, through the establishment of the British Empire, and technologically, with innovations like the steam engine, the industrial weaving machine and more. It was the era of the First Industrial Revolution.

The 'British' Industrial Revolution made for a fantastic twin engine of global trade. On the one hand, steamships and trains could transport goods over thousands of miles, both within countries and across countries. On the other hand, its industrialization allowed Britain to make products that were in demand all over the world, like iron, textiles and manufactured goods. 'With its advanced industrial technologies,' the BBC recently wrote, looking back to the era, 'Britain was able to attack a huge and rapidly expanding international market.'

The resulting globalisation was obvious in the numbers. For about a century, trade grew on average 3% per year. That growth rate propelled exports from a share of 6% of global GDP in the early 19th century, to 14% on the eve of World War I. As John Maynard Keynes, the economist, observed: 'The inhabitant of London could order by telephone, sipping his morning tea in bed, the various products of the whole Earth, in such quantity as he might see fit, and reasonably expect their early delivery upon his doorstep.'

And, Keynes also noted, a similar situation was also true in the world of investing. Those with the means in New York, Paris, London or Berlin could also invest in internationally active joint stock companies. One of those, the French Compagnie de Suez, constructed the Suez Canal, connecting the Mediterranean with the Indian Ocean and opened yet another artery of world trade. Others built railways in India, or managed mines in African colonies. Foreign direct investment, too, was globalizing.

While Britain was the country that benefited most from this globalisation, as it had the most capital and technology, others did too, by exporting other goods. The invention of the refrigerated cargo ship or 'reefer ship' in the 1870s, for example, allowed for countries like Argentina and Uruguay, to enter their golden age. They started to mass export meat, from cattle grown on their vast lands. Other countries, too, started to specialize their production in those fields in which they were most competitive.

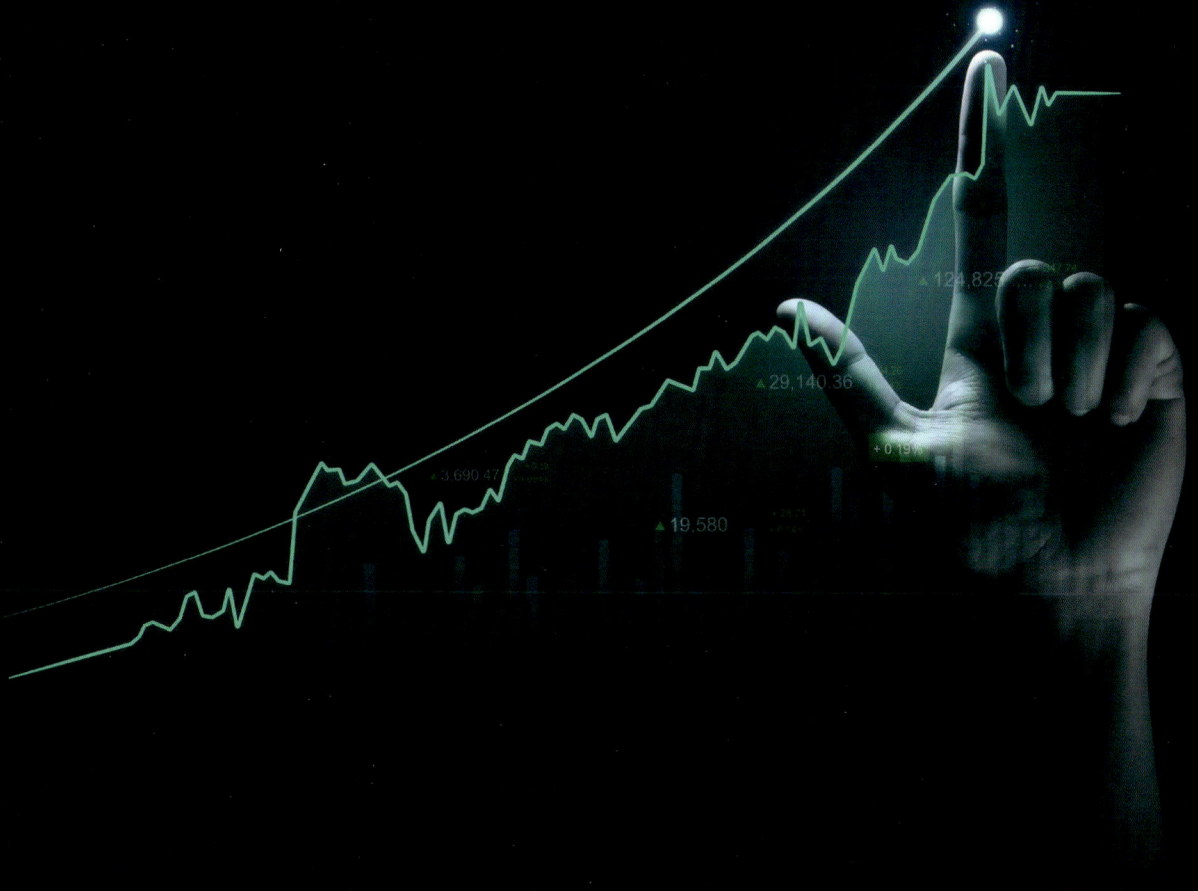

But the first wave of globalisation and industrialization also coincided with darker events, too. By the end of the 19th century, the Khan Academy notes, 'most [globalizing and industrialized] European nations grabbed for a piece of Africa, and by 1900 the only independent country left on the continent was Ethiopia'. In a similarly negative vein, large countries like India, China, Mexico or Japan, which were previously powers to reckon with, were either not able or not allowed to adapt to the industrial and global trends. Either the Western powers put restraints on their independent development, or they were otherwise outcompeted because of their lack of access to capital or technology. Finally, many workers in the industrialized nations also did not benefit from globalisation, their work commoditized by industrial machinery, or their output undercut by foreign imports.

The world wars

It was a situation that was bound to end in a major crisis, and it did. In 1914, the outbreak of World War I brought an end to just about everything the burgeoning high society of the West had gotten so used to, including globalisation. The ravage was complete. Millions of soldiers died in battle, millions of civilians died as collateral damage, war replaced trade, destruction replaced construction, and countries closed their borders yet again.

In the years between the world wars, the financial markets, which were still connected in a global web, caused a further breakdown of the global economy and its links. The Great Depression in the US led to the end of the boom in South America, and a run on the banks in many other parts of the world. Another world war followed in 1939-1945. By the end of World War II, trade as a percentage of world GDP had fallen to 5% – a level not seen in more than a hundred years.

Second and third wave of globalisation

The story of globalisation, however, was not over. The end of World War II marked a new beginning for the global economy. Under the leadership of a new hegemon, the United States of America, and aided by the technologies of the Second Industrial Revolution, like the car and the plane, global trade started to rise once again. At first, this happened in two separate tracks, as the Iron Curtain divided the world into two spheres of influence. But as of 1989, when the Iron Curtain fell, globalisation became a truly global phenomenon.

In the early decades after World War II, institutions like the European Union and other free trade vehicles championed by the US were responsible for much of the increase in international trade. In the Soviet Union, there was a similar increase in trade, albeit through centralized planning rather than the free market. The effect was profound. Worldwide, trade once again rose to 1914 levels: in 1989, export once again counted for 14% of global GDP. It was paired with a steep rise in middle-class incomes in the West.

Then, when the wall dividing East and West fell in Germany, and the Soviet Union collapsed, globalisation became an all-conquering force. The newly created World Trade Organization (WTO) encouraged nations all over the world to enter into free-trade agreements, and most of them did, including many newly independent ones. In 2001, even China, which for the better part of the 20th century had been a secluded, agrarian economy, became a member of the WTO, and started to manufacture for the world. In this 'new' world, the US set the tone and led the way, but many others benefited in their slipstream.

At the same time, a new technology from the Third Industrial Revolution, the internet, connected people all over the world in an even more direct way. The orders Keynes could place by phone in 1914 could now be placed over the internet. Instead of having them delivered in a few weeks, they would arrive at one's doorstep in a few days. What was more, the internet also allowed for a further global integration of value chains. You could do R&D in one country, sourcing in others, production in yet another, and distribution all over the world.

The result has been a globalisation on steroids. In the 2000s, global exports reached a milestone, as they rose to about a quarter of global GDP. Trade, the sum of imports and exports, consequentially grew to about half of world GDP. In some countries, like Singapore, Belgium, or others, trade is worth much more than 100% of GDP. A majority of global population has benefited from this: more people than ever before belong to the global middle class, and hundred of millions achieved that status by participating in the global economy.

Globalisation 4.0

That brings us to today, when a new wave of globalisation is once again upon us. In a world increasingly dominated by two global powers, the US and China, the new frontier of globalisation is the cyber world. The digital economy, in its infancy during the third wave of globalisation, is now becoming a force to reckon with through e-commerce, digital services, 3D printing. It is further enabled by artificial intelligence, but threatened by cross-border hacking and cyberattacks.

At the same time, a negative globalisation is expanding too, through the global effect of climate change. Pollution in one part of the world leads to extreme weather events in another. And the cutting of forests in the few 'green lungs' the world has left, like the Amazon rainforest, has a further devastating effect on not just the world's biodiversity, but its capacity to cope with hazardous greenhouse gas emissions.

But as this new wave of globalisation is reaching our shores, many of the world's people are turning their backs on it. In the West particularly, many middle-class workers are fed up with a political and economic system that resulted in economic inequality, social instability, and – in some countries – mass immigration, even if it also led to economic growth and cheaper products. Protectionism, trade wars and immigration stops are once again the order of the day

in many countries.

As a percentage of GDP, global exports have stalled and even started to go in reverse slightly. As a political ideology, 'globalism', or the idea that one should take a global perspective, is on the wane. And internationally, the power that propelled the world to its highest level of globalisation ever, the United States, is backing away from its role as policeman and trade champion of the world.

It was in this world that Chinese president Xi Jinping addressed the topic globalisation in a speech in Davos in January 2017. 'Some blame economic globalisation for the chaos in the world,' he said. 'It has now become the Pandora's box in the eyes of many.' But, he continued, 'we came to the conclusion that integration into the global economy is a historical trend. [It] is the big ocean that you cannot escape from.' He went on to propose a more inclusive globalisation, and to rally nations to join in China's new project for international trade, 'Belt and Road'.

It was in this world, too, that Alibaba a few months later opened its Silk Road headquarters in Xi'an. It was meant as the logistical backbone for the e-commerce giant along the new 'Belt and Road', the Paper reported. But if the old Silk Road thrived on the exports of luxurious silk by camel and donkey, the new Alibaba Xi'an facility would be enabling a globalisation of an entirely different kind. It would double up as a big data college for its Alibaba Cloud services.

Technological progress, like globalisation, is something you can't run away from, it seems. But it is ever changing. So how will Globalisation 4.0 evolve? We will have to answer that question in the coming years.

17 January 2019

Is the world retracting from globalisation, setting it up for a fifth wave?

An article from The Conversation.

By Elsabe Loots, Professor of Economics and former Dean of the Faculty of Economic and Management Sciences, University of Pretoria

Over the past 25 years there has been lots of research and debate about the concept, the history and state of globalisation, its various dimensions and benefits.

The World Economic Forum has set out the case that the world has experienced four waves of globalisation. In a 2019 publication it summarised them as follows.

The first wave is seen as the period since the late 19th century, boosted by the industrial revolution associated with the improvements in transportation and communication, and ended in 1914. The second wave commenced after WW2 in 1945 and ended in 1989. The third commenced with the fall of the Berlin Wall in 1989 and the disbanding of the former Soviet Union in 1991, and ended with the global financial crises in 2008.

The fourth wave kicked off in 2010 with the recovery of the impact of the global financial crises, the rising of the digital economy, artificial intelligence and, among others, the increasing role of China as a global powerhouse.

More recent debates on the topic focus on whether the world is now experiencing a retraction from the fourth wave and whether it is ready for the take-off of the fifth wave.

The similarities between the retraction period of the first wave and the current global dynamics a century later are startling. But do these similarities mean that a retraction from globalisation is evident? Is there sufficient evidence of de-globalisation or rather 'slowbalisation'?

Parallels

The drawn-out retreat from globalisation during the 30-year period – 1914 to 1945 – was characterised by the geopolitical and economic impact of WWI and WWII. Other factors were the 1918-1920 Spanish Flu pandemic; the Stock Market Crash of 1929 followed by the Great Depression of the 1930s; and the rise of the Communist Bloc under Stalin in the 1940s.

This period was further typified by protectionist sentiments, increases in tariffs and other trade barriers and a general retraction in international trade.

Looking at the current global context, the parallels are remarkable. The world is still fighting the COVID pandemic that had devastating effects on the world economy, global supply chains and people's lives and well-being.

For its part, the Russia-Ukraine war has caused major global uncertainties and food shortages. It has also led to increases in gas and fuel prices, further disruptions in global value chains and political polarisation.

The increase in the price of various consumer goods and in energy have put pressure on the general price level. World inflation is aggressively on the rise for the first time in 40 years. Monetary authorities worldwide are trying to fight inflation.

Global governance institutions like the World Trade Organization and the UN, which functioned well in the post-

WWII period, now have less influence while the Russian-Ukraine war has split the world politically into three groups. They are the Russian invasion supporters, the neutral countries and those opposing, a group dominated by the US, EU and the UK. This split is contributing to complex geopolitical challenges, which are slowly leading to changes in trade partnerships and regionalism.

Europe is already looking for new suppliers for oil and gas and early indications of the potential expansion of the Chinese influence in Asia are evident.

A less connected world

De-globalisation is seen as:

a movement towards a less connected world, characterised by powerful nation states, local solutions and border controls rather than global institutions, treaties, and free movement.

There's now talk of slowbalisation. The term was first used by trendwatcher and futurologist Adjiedji Bakas in 2015 to describe the phenomenon as the:

continued integration of the global economy via trade, financial and other flows, albeit at a significant slower pace.

The data on economic globalisation paint an interesting picture. They show that, even before the COVID pandemic hit the world in 2020, a deceleration in the intensity of globalisation is evident. The data which represent broad measures of globalisation, include:

World exports of goods and services. As a percentage of world GDP, these reached an all-time high of 31% in 2008 at the end of the third globalisation wave. Exports fell as a percentage of global GDP and only recovered to that level during the early stages of the fourth wave in 2011. Exports then slowly started to regress to 28% of global GDP in 2019 and further to a low of 26% during the first Covid-19 year in 2020.

The volume of foreign direct investment inflows. These reached a peak of US$2 trillion in 2016 before trending lower, reaching US$1.48 trillion in 2019. Although the 2020 foreign direct investment inflows of US$963 billion are a staggering 20% below the 2009 financial crises level, they recovered to US$1.58 billion in 2021.

Foreign direct investment as percentage of GDP started to increase from a mere 1% in 1989 to a peak of 5,3% in 2007. After a retraction following the global financial crises, it peaked again in 2015 and 2016 at around 3,5%. It then declined to 1,7% in 2019 and 1,4% in 2020.

Multinational enterprises have been the major vehicle for economic globalisation over time. The number of them indicates the willingness of companies to invest outside their home countries. In 2008 the UN Conference on Trade and Development reported approximately 82 000. The number declined to 60 000 in 2017.

Data on world private capital flows (including foreign direct investment, portfolio equity flows, remittances and private sector borrowing) are not readily available. However, Organisation for Economic Co-operation and Development

data show that private capital flows for reporting countries reached an all-time high of US$414 billion in 2014, followed by a declining trend to US$229 billion in 2019 and a negative outflow of US$8 billion in 2020.

These declining trends are further substantiated by the evidence of deeper fragmentation in economic relations caused by Brexit and the problematic US/China relations, in particular during the Trump era.

What next?

The question now is whether the latest data is:

- indicative of either a retraction from globalisation similar to that experienced after the first wave a century ago;
- or it is merely a process of de-globalisation;
- or slowbalisation in anticipation of the world economy's recovery from the impact of Covid-19 pandemic and the war in Ukraine?

The similarities between the first wave of globalisation and the existing global events are certainly significant, although embedded in a total different world order.

The current dynamics shaping the world such as the advancement of technology, the digital era and the speed with which technology and information is spread, will certainly influence the intensity of the retraction of the already embedded dependence on globalisation.

Nation states realise that blindly entering into contracts and agreements with companies in other countries may be problematic and that trade and investment partners need to be chosen carefully. The events over the past three years have certainly shown that economies around the world are deeply integrated and, despite examples of protectionism and threats of more inward-looking policies, it will not be possible to retract in totality.

What may occur is fragmentation where supply chains become more regionalised. Nobel prize winning economist Joseph Stiglitz refers to the move to 'friend shoring' of production, a phrase coined by US Treasury Secretary Janet Yellen.

It is becoming obvious that the process of globalisation certainly shows characteristics of both de-globalisation and slowbalisation. It's also clear that the global external shocks require a total rethink, repurpose and reform of the process of globalisation. This will most probably lead the world into the fifth wave of globalisation.

21 July 2022

Globalisation is in crisis. Here's how we can make it work for all

For the open global economy to survive, losers from technological change and trade must be compensated.

By Bernice Lee

Just as climate change worsens existing vulnerabilities such as food poverty and water shortages, trade amplifies weaknesses in the social fabric. In regions where people have fallen behind economically due to political neglect and technological change, it is jobs lost in the face of import competition that make the headlines. The appeal of Donald Trump and Brexit had much to do with deep grievances felt by those attributing their social problems to the negative impacts of openness and competition from shores afar.

Yet the costs of doing away with globalisation and our open-trading system could far exceed any benefits. This is why, in 2021, the World Trade Organization (WTO) will begin its metamorphosis into an organisation that puts social issues at its heart.

Economics 101 posits that trade creates winners and losers, but with all countries gaining overall. The economists were, and still are, right about this. Where they fell short was to assume that redistribution would happen. This now looks like magical thinking of the trickle-down era.

For the open global economy to survive, losers from technological change and trade must be compensated and empowered to benefit from new market conditions. The alternative will be to give up trade, which is a proven way for countries to earn hard currency that could help reduce poverty or secure critical supplies amid, for example, pandemics.

International institutions are often slow to change and the paralysis at the WTO has been exacerbated by US-China geopolitical strife. But in 2021 we will acknowledge that the benefits of global trade are still not felt where they are needed most. The viability of the multilateral trading system now depends on its ability to reduce pain on the economic margins of advanced economies, and tackle trade's discontents head-on.

To do this, member states will be asked to evaluate and report on their trade readiness not only from the economic vantage point of trade distortions, but also from the point of view of social dimensions. This will force politicians to be more honest about the gains and losses from trade and also about their distribution. It will also encourage more responsible action regarding supply chains, something we are already seeing in California, for example, with the Transparency in Supply Chains Act, which seeks to reduce modern slavery.

Closing borders would create new winners and losers, just as open markets have. The WTO cannot change this equation, but it can promote a more honest discourse on trade and encourage better use of domestic policies to mitigate social ills. It will also be able to lead in the establishment of a new global fund to address social-justice issues around trade and equity.

Globalisation is in crisis and its future depends on a renegotiation of the social contract. Trade is now a weapon of choice for many politicians, but we know from multiple surveys that younger generations are loath to forego concerns over equality, labour rights, the environment and gender parity. In 2021, the WTO will be key to placing social concerns at the heart of our debates about globalisation.

Bernice Lee is the executive director of the Hoffmann Centre for Sustainable Resource Economy

10 February 2021

Brainstorm

Make a list of the benefits of global trade. Can you think of any that aren't mentioned in this article?

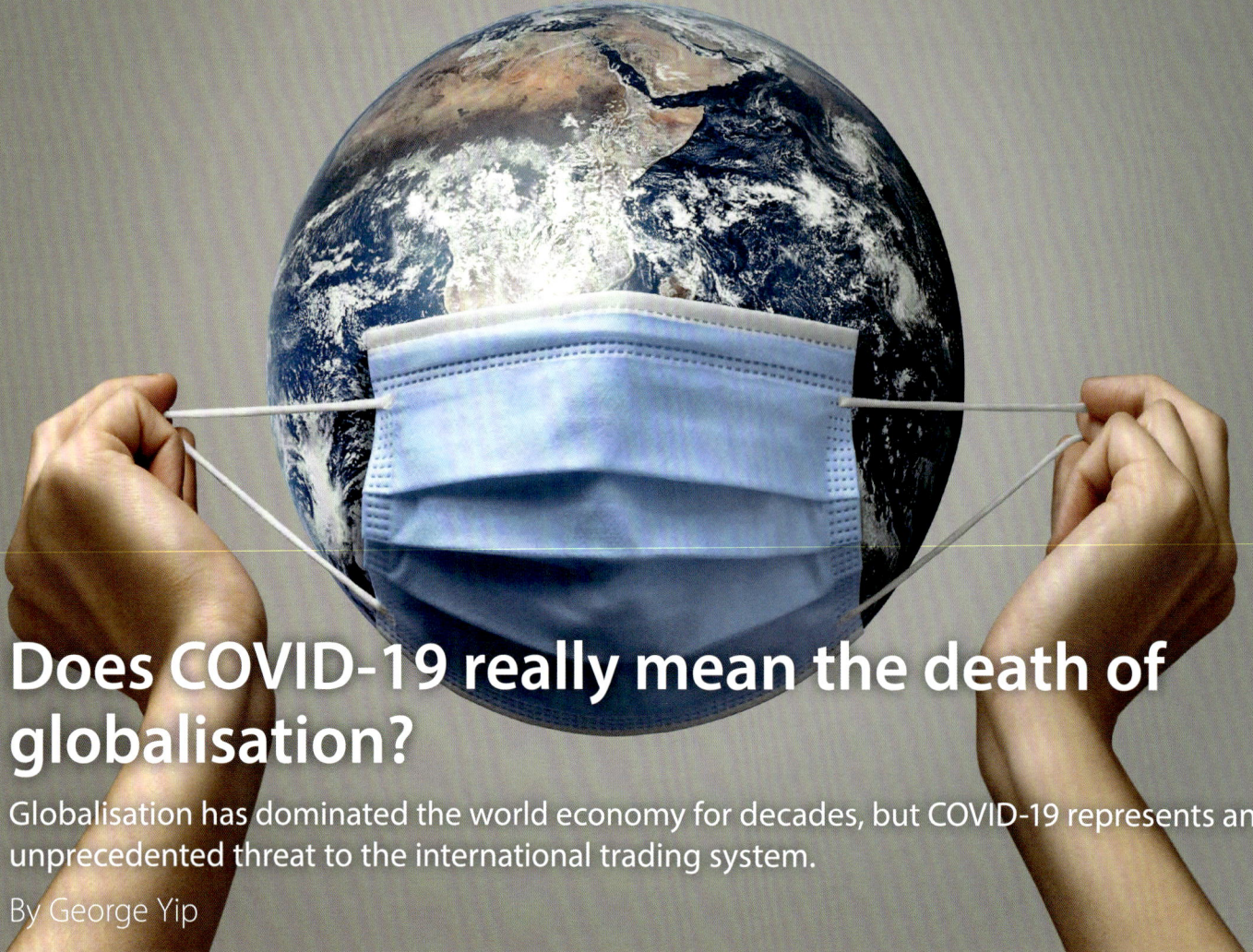

Does COVID-19 really mean the death of globalisation?

Globalisation has dominated the world economy for decades, but COVID-19 represents an unprecedented threat to the international trading system.

By George Yip

For a long time, the globalisation of business was accelerated by key geopolitical events: the gradual opening of China from 1979, the fall of the Berlin Wall in 1989, and the formations of the European Union in 1993 and of NAFTA in 1994, to name just a few.

Since then, the unequal distribution of the rewards and costs of globalisation, especially within developed countries, has led to two major political events that have started to reverse certain aspects of this system: the election of US President Donald Trump – a protectionist and anti-internationalist leader – and the United Kingdom's vote to leave the European Union, both in 2016.

'COVID-19 is probably the greatest peacetime disruptor of globalisation in the history of the modern world'

Other phenomena have also triggered calls for the reversal of globalisation. For example, when the price of oil peaked at $147 a barrel in 2008, companies briefly sought to deglobalise their supply chains as transportation costs were becoming too high.

Now we have COVID-19, probably the greatest disruptor of globalisation in the history of the modern world – except for the two world wars.

A lasting threat?

When considering whether COVID-19 will have a permanent effect on the strategies of multinational companies, the answer depends, of course, on how long it lasts, as well as the continuing threat of future pandemics.

The effect of COVID-19 on globalisation strategies comes via four mechanisms: the behaviour of national governments, the attitudes of consumers, the mindset of executives and key stakeholders in multinational companies, and the economics of business globalisation.

'Voters may be against free trade in theory, but they support it with their wallets'

Before COVID-19, China put itself forward as the champion of free trade at the World Economic Forum in Davos. Many observers were surprised. But in the history of international trade, it has always been the country with international competitive advantages that has adopted this attitude. First it was Britain, then the United States, and now it is the turn of China.

However, some national governments may use COVID-19 as an excuse to pull back from multilateralism and free trade, leaving them in an interesting position with voters.

This is because voters may be against free trade in theory but they support it with their wallets when they shop. Walmart, the largest retail chain in the United States, continues to source 70-80 per cent of its products from Chinese suppliers. Occasional calls for boycotts have gone nowhere and this is unlikely to change. After all, the 'Walmart Woman' (my US equivalent of Britain's 'Mondeo Man') wants the best bargains for her family.

Commitment vs. flexibility

Meanwhile, for multinational companies it is a straightforward choice between commitment and flexibility. Commitment to specialised supply chains based on the smallest number of lowest cost countries that can provide the required quality levels, yields the greatest short-term profit.

Of course, such a strategy also poses high risks, especially in the face of 'Black Swan' disruptions. So, all companies build in some duplication and flexibility in their global supply chains, including to guard against putting themselves into adverse bargaining positions but the cost of duplication and flexibility can be high.

'Companies that sacrifice short-term profits for greater long-term security suffer the risk of hostile takeovers'

On this issue, a stakeholder view of the multinational company can give us a better understanding of what companies will do.

The manager or director charged with designing and running a global supply chain is always under huge profit pressure to deliver in the cheapest and most efficient way. This profit pressure continues up the hierarchy all the way to the chief executive. Remember how the BP Deepwater Horizon oil spill in 2010 is often attributed to cost cutting due to top down pressure from the highest levels of the company.

Managing global supply chains

It is probably only boards of directors who can apply counter pressures for more flexible and secure supply chains. But companies that sacrifice short-term profits for greater long-term security then suffer the risk of hostile takeovers.

This is particularly the case in the United States and the United Kingdom, with their so-called 'Anglo-Saxon' system

Key Facts

- 1979 - the gradual opening of China
- 1989 - the fall of the Berlin Wall
- 1993 - the European Union was formed
- 2016 - the UK voted to leave the EU
- 2019 - the emergence of COVID-19
- 2020 - the UK left the EU

of corporate governance that greatly prioritises the interests of current shareholders (the vast majority of holdings being for months rather than years).

'More profitable companies will be able to afford the short-term cost of making their supply chains more flexible'

For this reason, I predict that companies based in mainland Europe or in Asia, which give more protection to companies relative to shareholders, or private companies, will be more likely to create more flexible global supply chains.

My other prediction is that larger, more profitable companies will be able to afford the short-term cost of making their supply chains more flexible. This reflects how these types of companies are leading in other initiatives, such as sustainability – they have the means to introduce changes for the long-term gain of both the company and the world.

5 August 2020

Coronavirus hasn't killed globalisation – it proves why we need it

An article from The Conversation.

By Sunil Venaik, Associate Professor of International Business, The University of Queensland

In just a few months, COVID-19 travelled from China to more than 200 other countries, and has now killed more than 200,000 people. Some claim the pandemic sounds the death knell for globalisation – but in fact, it reveals the disasters that can arise when nations try to go it alone.

Examining where the world went right or wrong in its COVID-19 response may help mitigate another global crisis, climate change.

In the face of coronavirus' global sweep, most national governments acted independently from each other, rather than in unison. Just as in global action on climate change, the responses of nations to the health crisis has largely been ad hoc, piecemeal and, in many cases, lethally ineffective.

My recent research as an international business scholar has focused on finding the common threads of national cultures. My research shows that people around the world have many needs and aspirations in common, such as good health, education and employment. These are best fulfilled when world leaders work jointly with a global, rather than a national, mindset.

So let's look at the lessons COVID-19 has taught the world, and how this might help the global effort to curb climate change.

Disunity is death

Following the COVID-19 outbreak in China, many countries imposed unilateral travel bans on Chinese arrivals, against advice from the World Health Organization.

The bans mirror the response of many nations during the west African Ebola epidemic which began in 2013. Research has shown that those travel and trade restrictions acted as a disincentive for nations to report outbreaks.

There are undoubtedly legitimate questions over China's reporting on the coronavirus outbreak. However, travel bans may have made China more defensive and less willing to share vital information with the rest of the world.

A shortage of vital supplies also exposed fractures in international cooperation. For example, France and Germany banned the export of medical equipment such as face masks, and the United States was accused of intercepting a shipment of medical supplies en route to Germany.

But where the world has cooperated to stop the spread of COVID-19, the benefits have been obvious. Collaboration between global health scientists has helped identify the virus' genome sequence, and grow the virus in the lab.

Similarly on climate change, international unity is required if the world is to keep temperatures below 2° warming this century. But international climate meetings frequently end in disunity and despair. Meanwhile, global emissions creep ever higher.

The butterfly effect

One person practising social distancing during the pandemic might think their effect is negligible. But coronavirus is highly infectious: on one estimate, a single person with coronavirus could eventually infect 59,000 others.

Similarly, many countries seek to avoid responsibility for taking climate action by claiming their contribution to the global problem is small. The Australian government, for example, repeatedly points out it contributes just 1.3% to the world's emissions total.

But on a per capita basis, Australia is one of the world's highest emitters. And as a rich, developed nation, we must be seen to be taking action on cutting emissions if poorer nations are expected to follow suit. So actions Australia takes will have major global consequences.

Act quickly

In the two months it took the virus to spread from China and become a global pandemic, other nations could have readied themselves by amassing test kits, ventilators and personal protective equipment. But many nations did not adequately prepare.

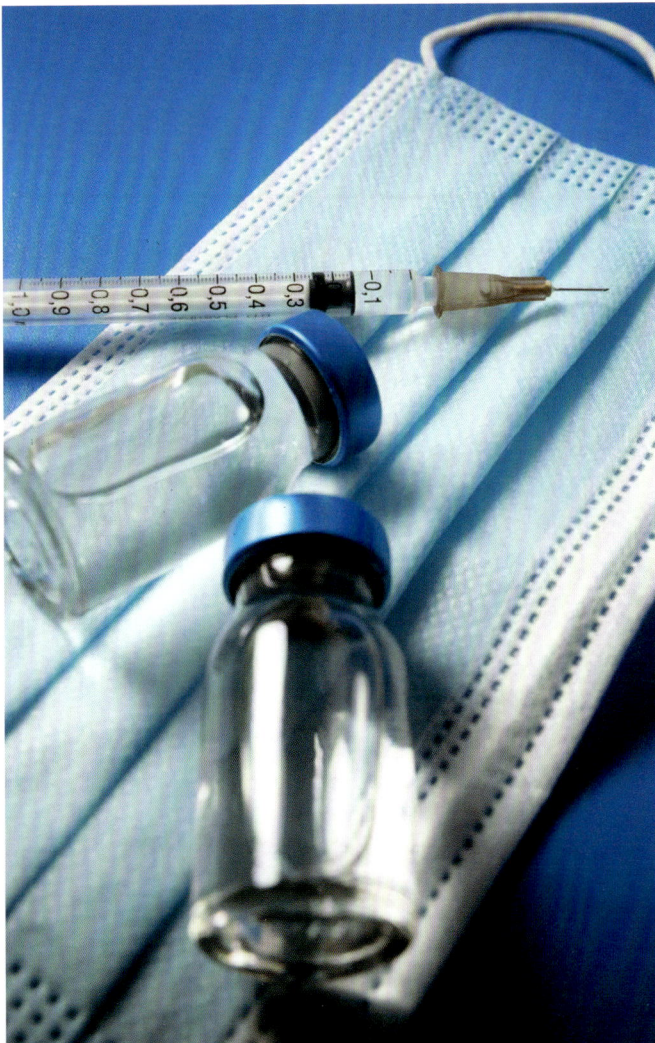

For example the US was slow to implement a widespread testing regime, and Japan did not declare a nationwide state of emergency until mid-April.

Of course the world has had a far longer time to adapt to and mitigate climate change. The time lag between emissions and their consequences is years, even centuries. There has been ample opportunity to take progressive and thoughtful corrective action against climate change. Instead, the crisis has been met with complacency.

As the COVID-19 experience has shown, the longer we delay action on climate mitigation, the more global, costly, and lethal the consequences.

Challenges ahead

As others have noted, a major supplier of swabs used for coronavirus testing is based in Italy, and a German company is a primary supplier of chemicals needed for the tests. Many countries rely on foreign suppliers for ventilators, and an Indian firm – the world's largest vaccine manufacturer – says once a COVID-19 vaccine is ready for mass production, it will supply large volumes to the world, at low cost.

It's clear that international cooperation is critical for effective mass testing and treatment for the virus. Nations must work together to improve production and distribution, and resources must be shared.

So too is cooperation needed to deal with the worldwide economic downturn. The global recovery will be long and slow if nations adopt sovereign mindsets, putting up barriers to protect their own economies.

With the coronavirus as with climate change, working together is best way to secure humanity's safety, health and well-being.

6 May 2020

Why the world needs better – not less – globalisation

By Ian Goldin, Professor of Globalisation and Development; Director, Oxford Martin Programme on Technological and Economic Change, Oxford Martin School, University of Oxford & Robert Muggah, Co-founder, SecDev Group and Co-founder, Igarapé Institute

- **Globalisation entails the spreading of new forms of risk, just as it brings benefits.**

- **Given mishandlings of the pandemic, the decline of Atlantic trade relative to the rise in Pacific and Indian Ocean trade will be more rapid than foreseen.**

- **The current inability of politicians to manage global threats and build a more inclusive world is a sign of too little globalisation, not too much.**

Globalisation is the most progressive force in the history of humankind. It has heralded more rapid improvements to more people than any other human intervention. While COVID-19 has temporarily disrupted some cogs in the chains of moving goods, services, people and – to a lesser extent ideas – that constitutes globalisation, it has accelerated others.

The pandemic offers a once-in-a-lifetime opportunity to reset globalisation to ensure that the benefits are more widely shared and the threats it compounds – pandemics, climate change, inequality and so on – are greatly reduced.

Unless globalisation's dark side is tackled head on, the rise in systemic risk and increasing political pushback will lead to deglobalisation. This would mean less multilateral cooperation to address critical global challenges and a poorer, less inclusive and more unsustainable world.

Globalisation accelerated in the late 1980s and early '90s with the collapse of the Soviet bloc, the opening up of China, the integration of Europe and NAFTA in North America, and the Uruguay Round trade negotiations which halved tariffs globally.

At the same time, the development of the World Wide Web was ushering in the digital age.

Globalisation isn't perfect

One of the results over the past three decades was a doubling in the average per-capita income. In addition, 1.3 billion people have escaped desperate poverty, the average life expectancy globally has increased by about 10 years, and over 50 countries became democratic.

And yet, globalisation appears more unpopular than ever. We think that the principal reason is the butterfly defect of globalisation: the hyper-connectivity of increasingly complex systems leads to the spreading of new forms of risk as well as benefits.

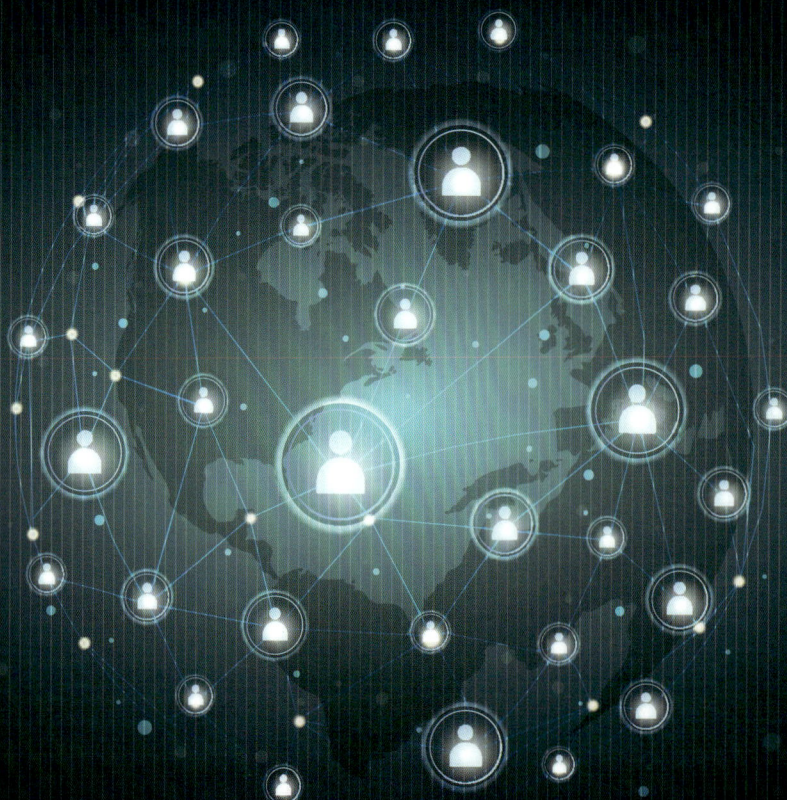

Major financial centres generate financial opportunities, but networks of financial centres are also the source of financial contagion. Servers, fibre and cloud systems drive the digital economy, but also hasten the spread of digital viruses, fake news and misinformation.

While major airport hubs facilitate travel and logistics, they also encourage the flow of illicit goods and the spread of pandemics. Meanwhile, the success of globalisation also spawns new risks: more access to electricity and transport help carbon emissions soar; increased use of antibiotics improves health outcomes but simultaneously creates antibiotic resistance; and increasing consumption of plastics threatens the oceans.

How COVID-19 disrupted globalisation: the busts and the booms

COVID-19 has not derailed globalisation. On the contrary: it has accelerated its transformation. Some features of globalisation, such as scientific collaboration and digital connectivity, have increased dramatically since the pandemic began. The pandemic will also ultimately lead to a sharp increase in cross-border flows of capital, as over 100 countries seek financial support from international institutions and creditors.

We should expect, too, that the dramatic changes in the fortunes of different sectors and countries will precipitate a new wave of mergers and acquisitions.

The fragmentation of supply chains had already started peaking back in 2019, and COVID-19 has accelerated the trend.

Likewise, automation was busy shifting its comparative advantage away from low-cost, low-skilled locations towards major markets, where skills and machines are available.

And yet, it is not only manufacturing which is being automated; services are too, with digital payments and administrative processes now being located on cloud computers, negating any need for outsourcing to low-cost locations.

'Authentic experiences are becoming a more significant part of consumer spending as incomes increase, especially in Asia.' – Ian Goldin

All of this is being reinforced by customers demanding quick delivery, which is easy to achieve from nearby production centres but less so from distant factories. Meanwhile, politicians are reinforcing the call to bring production back home, but it is automated processes and skilled jobs – and not work in factories or service centres – that are setting up shop near the major markets.

This restructuring of supply chains and reshoring of services and manufacturing will not reverse globalisation. However, it will transform it. So too will the permanently lower growth of business travel as the efficiency, cost- and carbon-saving benefits of remote meetings mean digital flows will replace physical travel.

Foreign travel for leisure and tourism purposes will, however, rebound once vaccines are widely distributed, as authentic experiences become a more significant part of consumer spending and incomes increase, especially in Asia.

The globalisation of the future will centre on East Asia, which accounts for half of the world's population and is the fastest-growing economic region. The rapid recovery of this region from the COVID-19 crisis and the November 2020 Regional Comprehensive Economic Partnership of 14 Asia-Pacific economies will reinforce its rising economic and political power.

Global trade in manufactured goods

Our drastically changing political and economic landscape has led to a transitional period in which there is no effective global, much less multilateral, leadership. International institutions are being starved of the resources, legitimacy and mandates for reform that they urgently require.

The lack of political will to manage global threats and build a more inclusive world is the greatest challenge facing globalisation, a point frequently made by the UN Secretary General António Guterres. In this respect, there is too little globalisation, not too much.

'Globalisation needs better management. The failure to manage increased flows across national borders is what gives rise to crises.' – Robert Muggah

International firms operate seamlessly across national borders but are becoming the victims of increasingly nationalist politics. This threatens to undermine investment and the shared understanding that is vital to address our shared threats.

Ultimately, globalisation needs better management, and the failure to manage increased flows across national borders is what gave rise to the financial crisis, climate change and COVID-19.

Turning our back on globalisation is not the answer. Nor should we wish to bounce back to the pre-pandemic ways of doing things, as it is that type of business as usual that brought us the pandemic and much more dangerous threats such as climate change. It is unsustainable.

There is no wall high enough to keep out climate change, pandemics, nuclear Armageddon or any of the other grave threats we face. But high walls also keep out the investments, trade, people, technologies and building blocks of cooperation that are urgently needed to address threats, stimulate job creation and fuel growth.

COVID-19 has taught us that we need to redouble our efforts to create a more inclusive, more sustainable and healthier world in which globalisation serves to overcome risks and social divides, and is a tool for achieving shared and sustainable prosperity for all of humanity.

14 December 2020

Why will Globalisation prevail? The enduring forces and enablers

By Professor Graham Squires

In discussing globalisation, the term can be described as the convergence of markets, economies and ways of life across the world. A broad overview definition here is that globalisation is the worldwide process of homogenising prices, products, wages, rates of interest and profits. The important point to note here is globalisation as a process (a series of actions, changes or functions) rather than as a static stage of development. So as a 'process' of development, globalisation processes will rely on three forces for development at various scales (e.g. individual, household, urban spaces, national boundaries). The three forces for development in the process of globalisation are as follows:

- the role of human migration;

- international trade;

- rapid movements of capital and the integration of financial markets.

First, the role of human migration in globalisation is the way in which humans are, in general, freer to move between different jobs, spaces and nations. For instance, people can more quickly move to overseas jobs or encounter quicker commutes with the expansion of air travel (post-Covid-19) and the internet (for virtual and remote working). Migratory forces enable globalisation to develop as a more mobile workforce will mean a more efficient workforce and the ability to make economic gains.

The second force of international trade has had an impact on globalisation in that it is now easier than ever before to trade internationally. For example, the relaxation of employment regulations and the expansion of free(r) trading areas (such as the EU) has meant that a greater number of employees are able to work within different countries without having to spend time getting work permits.

The force of individuals and organisations wanting to trade internally is certainly a force that has encouraged globalisation, as greater trade will undoubtedly generate greater added value and thus economic satisfaction of wants. Thirdly, the rapid movement of capital and the integration of financial markets have had a significant influence as a force for globalisation.

The forces enacted by trading buyers and sellers of capital goods are to try to make such trading easier and more efficient. As such, this trading in capital goods and flows can be encouraged to flow without barriers between national frameworks. The force in this area is therefore the greater returns that can be extracted by traders in various global locations where capital has not previously had the opportunity to flourish.

As well as forces that have encouraged globalisation processes to intensify, there are other reasons or enablers that have made this intensification happen. Three key enablers for globalisation are:

- financial markets around the world becoming more integrated;

- technology and electronic trading in the value of commodities;

- money markets in one country not being independent of world financial markets.

The integration of financial markets around the world has played a significant role in enabling globalisation to intensify. The ability of, say, HSBC (Hongkong Shanghai Banking Corporation) to provide banking and financial services around the world is a case in point. HSBC is, for instance, the second-largest banking and financial services group and second-largest public company. As such it is listed on the London Stock Exchange and a constituent of the FTSE 100 index. As well as being integrated into the global financial system, it has managed to extend its reach by acquiring various banks in different countries. This acquisition is one of many integrations that enabled such a financial reach for HSBC and many other global financial organisations that operate in the global financial market. To get a sense of scale in this global financial reach, HSBC has around 7,500 offices in 87 countries and territories across Africa, Asia, Europe, North America and South America and around 100 million customers.

With respect to advances in technology and electronic trading, they have enabled globalisation to flourish, for instance, web technologies and the internet have made possible the processing of information more efficient across the globe. The creation of a virtual space in which people work and share information has meant that activities can take place over geography without people having to physically be in proximity.

As a third enabler, money markets have become more integrated with world financial markets to enable globalisation to occur. For instance, the trading of pounds, dollars, yen etc. as more liquid assets (money that can be exchanged for goods now rather than, say, bonds that can be redeemed in a few years) plays a larger role in the financial

markets as a whole if finance is hard to come by as seen in the financial crisis of 2007–08. The high demand for short-term borrowing and lending in money markets (one year or less), such as treasury bills, will mean that it has an effect on the global financial market of which money markets are a part.

What is of importance to globalisation is that this greater inter-connectedness of money and financial markets means that investments (in say property development for cities) can more quickly and easily be financed during economic growth over a global spread; but also, liquidity for credit in buying construction materials or property assets can quickly contract following wider global financial market falls (e.g. stock market crash). That in turn can quickly slow down or halt the economic development of many cities across the globe. As for a global pandemic, this is more a short term crisis of people rather than financial capital, and thus it can be argued that globalisation will prevail.

Summary

- Globalisation can be described as the convergence of markets, economies and ways of life across the world.

A broad overview definition is that globalisation is the worldwide process of homogenising prices, products, wages, rates of interest and profits.

- Globalisation is a process (a series of actions, changes or functions) rather than a static stage of development. So as a 'process' of development, globalisation will rely on three forces for development at various scales (e.g. individual, household, urban spaces and national boundaries).

- The three forces for development in the process of globalisation are: (1) the role of human migration; (2) the level of international trade; and (3) the rapid movements of capital and integration of financial markets.

- Three key enablers for globalisation are: (1) financial markets around the world that have become more integrated; (2) technology and electronic trading in the value of commodities; and (3) money markets in one country not being independent of world financial markets.

Activity

- Write a short definition for the term Globalisation.

- How are different places connected through globalisation?

- Which factors aid globalisation?

- What types of globalisation are there?

The above information is reprinted with kind permission from Professor Graham Squires.
© 2022 Professor Graham Squires

www.grahamsquires.com

Slowbalisation – is globalisation slowing down?

By Tejvan Pettinger

Slowbalisation – a phenomenon which involves a slowing down of the pace of global integration.

In recent decades globalisation has become so dominant that we often assume the process is never-ending. Between 1970 and 2008, world exports as a share of GDP rose from 13% to 31%, and it seemed that globalisation was an unstoppable force.

However, since 2008, something unexpected has happened. Exports as a share of GDP has flatlined and even started to fall. Other metrics show a similar fate, a fall in global bank loans, foreign direct investment has fallen quite sharply and multinational's share of profit has decreased.

Covid has further brought into question more aspects of globalisation, such as international travel.

Of course, we still live in a very globalised world, and other metrics such as – internet use, and international phone call measurements, globalisation continues to intensify. But, in terms of trade and the movement of people, we may have reached peak globalisation.

What factors are behind the slowdown in globalisation?

1. Gains from lower costs reached. From the 1960s, we saw a very sharp fall in transport costs, due to processes such as containerisation; this made trade much more profitable, but these 'easy' gains have been largely exhausted. Now transport faces higher costs from rising fossil fuel prices.

2. Improved technology. With labour-intensive industries there is a very clear incentive for firms to move production to countries with significantly lower costs. In the past, manufacturing firms in the US and Europe had a strong incentive to move manufacturing off-shore. However, as manufacturing processes become increasingly automated, labour costs will become a smaller share of total costs. In the future manufacturing will not rely on cheap, plentiful labour, but a more skilled workforce able to manage technology. Therefore the need to ship goods halfway around the world will not be there. Already there are examples of 'reshoring' Between 2008 and 2017, US manufacturing has created 16,000 jobs through reshoring.

3. Relative decline of manufacturing to services. As incomes rise, we tend to see higher growth for income elastic services rather than goods. For example, as incomes rise we spend more on beauty treatments, going out for restaurant meals and personal services. These services cannot obviously be imported from across the world in the same way goods are. Therefore, more of our income is going on local services compared to international goods.

4. Changing consumer preferences. In the past, many manufactured goods were identical. A firm would produce millions of goods on a large scale. However, the modern consumer is increasingly demanding a much more personalised product. Thirty years ago, if you wanted a chair, you would buy what you are

Global foreign direct investment

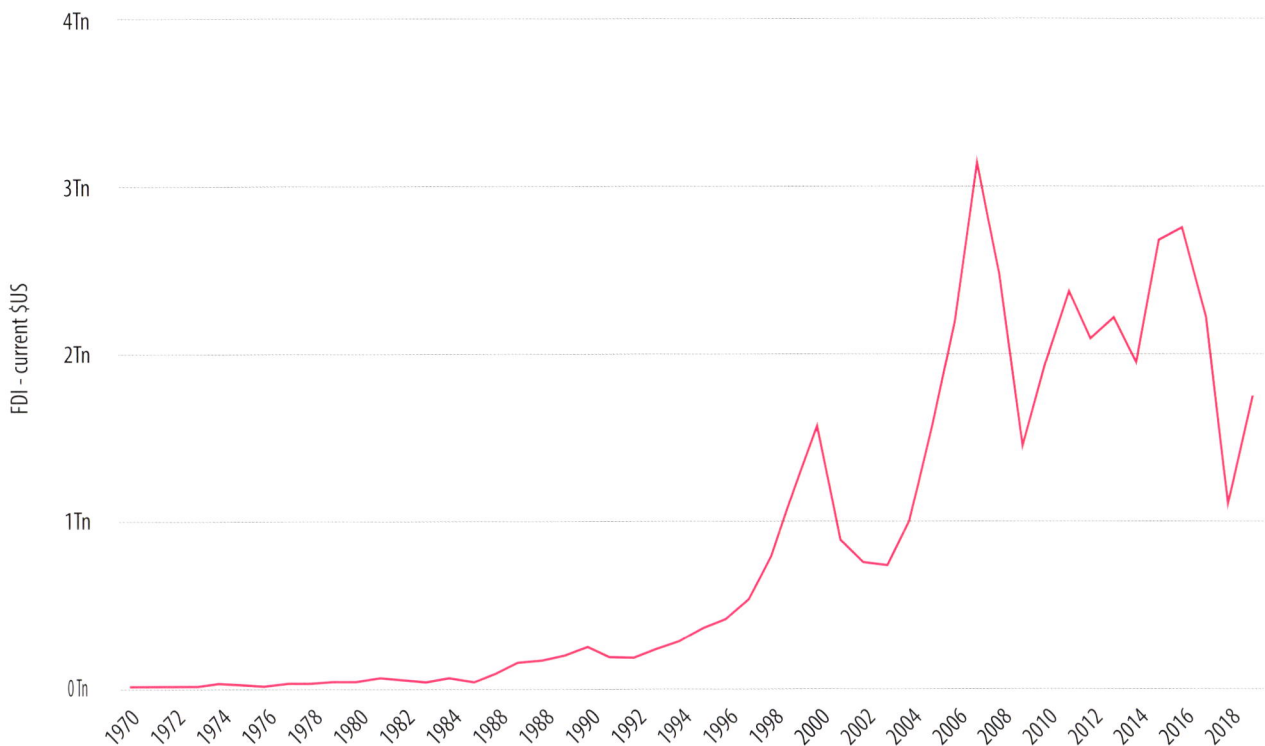

Source: World Bank - TBX.KLT.DINV.CD.WD - Accessed 4 September 2021

given. But, now a consumer can choose between 20-30 variations of colour and features. This means firms have an incentive to move production closer to where consumers live. If you have to wait three months for a shipping container to arrive from Asia, it is too long – consumer preferences may have changed. Successful firms will be based close to their retail market so that the highly individual products can be delivered quickly.

5. Higher tariffs. Free trade has created winners and losers. Overall there is a net economic welfare gain, but often the losers have been more visible, creating political pressure. Populists such as Trump have responded by placing higher tariffs on goods – challenging the assumption that tariffs would always fall. It is not just tariffs, but regional blocks are increasingly splintering on issues such as regulation, privacy requirements and tax policy.

6. Environmental concerns. In the past decade, environmental concerns such as the global imprint of products have become increasingly important. Consumers are increasingly wary about buying goods which are imported from the other side of the world, and are willing to pay a premium for goods and food sourced locally. Firms are also responding to this pressure by making some efforts to source locally.

7. Carbon taxes. Another factor that may feature in the future is higher taxes on carbon emissions which will increase the costs for aeroplane use and global shipping. Of course, the industry may find more environmentally friendly methods of transport, but electric engines are harder to use for shipping and planes.

8. Multinational firms have found their limits. Multinational firms have often found that global expansion is not without risks. If the multinational doesn't understand the local market, it can fail to replicate its domestic success. One example, Tesco and Marks and Spencer set up in France but failed to win over the French shopper and they had to retreat.

Globalisation isn't declining its changing

• Another way of looking at the situation is that globalisation is still occurring but it is changing. Rather than growth through trade of goods, we are seeing a growth in the diffusion of ideas, technology and some services. 10 years ago, if you wanted a print designer, you would find someone local, but now it is just as easy to employ a designer in Brazil or India.

• Covid has led to a slowdown in international travel, but we are still meeting with people around the world through Zoom and Skype.

• 20 years ago we bought computers, but now we spend more on data storage, apps and pdfs. This data storage and web-traffic is very much a global industry.

• Also, whilst trade in goods has flatlined, it is still just under 30% of GDP. Some industries, like car and steel manufacture, have such significant economies of scale, it is hard to envisage anything other than the global supply chains we see now.

9 September 2021

What if the world was one country? A psychologist on why we need to think beyond borders

An article from The Conversation.

By Steve Taylor, Senior Lecturer in Psychology, Leeds Beckett University

There are countless different species on the surface of this planet. One of these is the human race, which has over seven billion members. In one sense, there are no nations, just groups of humans inhabiting different areas of the planet. In some cases, there are natural borders formed by sea or mountains, but often borders between nations are simply abstractions, imaginary boundaries established by agreement or conflict.

Rusty Schweikhart, a member of the 1969 Apollo 9 space mission, explained how when he looked at the Earth from space, he experienced a profound shift in perspective. Like most of us, he was brought up to think in terms of countries with borders and different nationalities, but seeing the world from this new angle changed his view. He felt 'part of everyone and everything'. As he described it:

You look down there and you can't imagine how many borders and boundaries you cross, again and again and again, and you don't even see them.

Schweikhart's perspective reminds us that we belong to the Earth rather than to a nation, and to a species rather than a nationality. And although we might feel distinct and different, we all have a common source. Our species originally developed in eastern Africa around 200,000 years ago and migrated out into the rest of the world in a series of waves. If there was an ancestry website that could trace our lineage back to the very beginning, we would find that we all have the same great-great (followed by many other 'greats') grandparents.

How then do we explain nationalism? Why do humans separate themselves into groups and take on different national identities? Maybe different groups are helpful in terms of organisation, but that doesn't explain why we feel different. Or why different nations compete and fight with one another.

The psychological theory of 'terror management' offers one clue. This theory, which has been validated by many studies, shows that when people are made to feel insecure and anxious, they tend to become more concerned with nationalism, status and success. We seem to have an impulse to cling to labels of identity to defend ourselves against insecurity. There has, however, been criticism of the theory by some psychologists who believe it overlooks wider factors that contribute to human behaviour.

That said, the theory could go some way to help explain why nationalism grows in times of crisis and uncertainty. Poverty and economic instability often lead to increased nationalism and to ethnic conflict. An increased sense of insecurity brings a stronger need for conceptual labels to strengthen our sense of identity. We also feel the impulse to gain security through the feeling of belonging to a group with shared beliefs and conventions.

On this basis then it's likely that people who feel the strongest sense of separation and the highest levels of insecurity and anxiety are the most prone to nationalism, racism and to fundamentalist religion.

Beyond nationalism

One pertinent finding from my own research as a psychologist is that people who experience high levels of wellbeing (together with a strong sense of connection to others, or to the world in general) don't tend to have a sense of group identity.

I have studied many people who have undergone profound personal transformation following intense psychological turmoil, such as bereavement or a diagnosis of cancer. I sometimes refer to these people as 'shifters', since they appear to shift up to a higher level of human development. They undergo a dramatic form of 'post-traumatic growth'. Their lives become richer, more fulfilling and meaningful. They have a new sense of appreciation, a heightened awareness of their surroundings, a wider sense of perspective and more intimate and authentic relationships.

As I report in my book, *The Leap*, one of the common traits of 'shifters' is that they no longer define themselves in terms of nationality, religion or ideology. They no longer feel they are American or British, or a Muslim or a Jew. They feel the same kinship with all human beings. If they have any sense of identity at all, it's as global citizens, members of the human race and inhabitants of the planet Earth – beyond nationality or border. Shifters lose the need for group identity because they no longer feel separate and so have no sense of fragility and insecurity.

Why we need trans-nationalism

In my view, then, all nationalistic enterprises – such as 'America First' or Brexit – are highly problematic, as they are based on anxiety and insecurity, so inevitably create discord and division. And since nationalism contravenes the essential reality of human nature and human origins, such enterprises always turn out to be temporary. It's impossible to override the fundamental interconnectedness of the human race. At some point, it always reasserts itself.

Like the world itself, our most serious problems have no borders. Problems like the COVID-19 pandemic and climate change affect us collectively and so can only be solved collectively – from a trans-nationalist approach. Such issues can only be properly solved by viewing humans as one species, without borders or boundaries.

Ultimately, nationalism is a psychological aberration. We owe it our ancestors and to our descendants – and to the Earth itself – to move beyond it.

21 January 2021

THE CONVERSATION

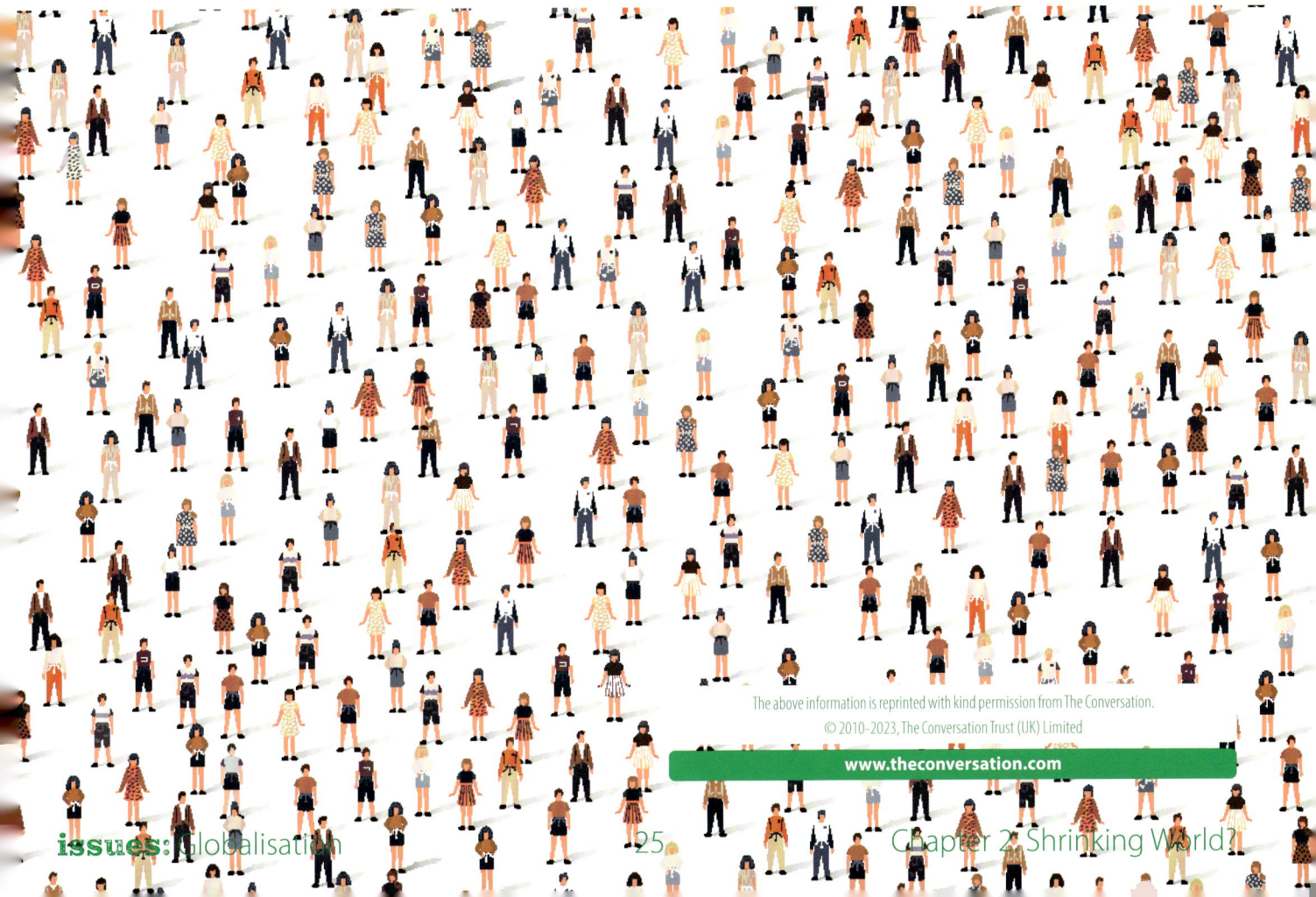

Diversity, waste, and travel: what globalisation means for food

Foreign, exotic foods have become staples in our households, but at what cost?

By Shreya Banerjee

For many people, being at home during lockdown means that there is an abundance of time to spend preparing, eating, and thinking about food. Combined with the population's increased dependence on home cooking due to the closure of restaurants, it seems there is no better time to consider where the products we label as essential originate from, the extent to which our diets have become international and the effects of this.

Food trade has played a significant role in the history of globalisation, as it has allowed for cultural exchange for thousands of years. From the transporting of spices along the Silk Road, to the potatoes being imported from the Andes to Ireland in 1589 by Sir Walter Raleigh, one could argue that humanity has been sharing and adapting to new crops for a very long time – after all, it took only 16 years for the potato to become widely farmed throughout Europe. But even if our swift adoption of and fascination for foreign crops dates back to Charles II being presented with a pineapple, the last century has undeniably ushered in a new age of consumption.

Where produce from far-off lands may once have radiated mystique, in today's world, over two thirds of the crops that underpin national diets are originally grown somewhere else. This is a trend that has accelerated dramatically over the last 50 years: whether it's sushi you're searching for in Addis Ababa or McDonald's in Honolulu, globalisation has made a wide range of cuisines more accessible than ever, while also aiding multinational fast food companies to exploit our modern need for convenience. It has not only transformed the produce that we eat and where it is grown, but also redefined our tastes internationally – interactions between different cultures as a result of immigration have led to an expectation of an Indian take-away in most British towns, and culinary phenomena such as Korean-Mexican fusion in Los Angeles and Japanese-Brazilian hybrid restaurants in London. Moreover, the popularity of cooking shows such as MasterChef, where contestants are encouraged to explore different cuisines, reflects how our society is more open to experimentation than ever before. Though this is of less relevance to communities that are dependent on livestock and backyard farming, urbanisation and immigration have created melting pots of cuisine and culture across the globe, which form perfect subjects for an inquiry into globalised diets.

Aside from being a vehicle for cultural metamorphosis, globalisation within the food industry has had major environmental effects, often inextricably bound to the politics of agriculture and trade, which are exacerbated by the ever-growing demand for food in an ever-growing population. The demand for meat across the globe has

never been higher, with countries such as Australia and the US consuming an average of over 300 grams per person, per day, and the largest increase has been for pork and chicken in Asia. This has led to expansion of pig meat farming that has raised currently pertinent concerns about public health and viruses, especially if farming is not regulated effectively.

Alongside the growth in demand for meat, the last decade has proven that wheat, soya beans and palm oil are 'megacrops': superpowers within agriculture with the potential to overhaul the productivity and value of land. In Brazil's Matopiba (the savannah region formed by several states which is the country's agricultural frontier) 14,000 sq km of native vegetation were cleared for soya cultivation from 2016-17 in order to satisfy the Chinese demand for soya beans – only to be left uncultivated by the U.S. because of the trade war between Beijing and Washington. The illegal deforestation and environmental endangerment that has resulted from a huge international demand for soya as well as palm oil is not dissimilar to what Mexico is experiencing from the avocado boom throughout the late 2010s, when the security of domestic produce was undermined by unparalleled Western demand for the incredibly Instagrammable toast-topper.

Clearly, the globalisation of our diets has had positive and negative effects – whilst many of us have access to a balanced diet that our ancestors could never have dreamt of and can taste delicious indigenous and fusion foods from around the world, there is an environmental cost. Having said this, it has also led to the increased accessibility and popularisation of veganism through new meat-free alternatives and the wide sharing of information on social media. A vegan diet can drastically reduce one's carbon footprint, but it is worth considering that most diets within a globally interdependent food supply chain quickly accumulate 'food miles', which is one factor used to measure the environmental impact of getting food from the farm to your fork.

Today, due to our growing consciousness of the impact that demand can have on an environment and its inhabitants,

as well as the pandemic having caused a large portion of our food supply chain to grind to a halt, food security seems to be higher on the agenda and more in the spotlight than ever. The rush to stockpile essential products has also provoked analysis of what we consider basic necessities, and it has become clear that although thousands of different foods are imported and exported every year, our global diet is starting to converge due to our dependence on a handful of megacrops, as well as the explosion of fast food culture in the last 50 years. Monocrop plantations of these megacrops such as corn, wheat and soya beans are more vulnerable to viruses and pests than plantations with biodiversity. However, in a world where cities have huge demand for key products and we are growing our own produce less, it may seem like there is no alternative to monocropping on a large scale.

Although the pandemic has propelled us into uncertain times, it can be comforting to satisfy our culinary curiosity by means of new recipes or the variety of restaurants still delivering food. Even when confined to our homes, globalisation has made it easier than ever to travel the world from our plates.

26 April 2020

Design

Design a poster about globalisation of food.

Pick either an international chain of restaurants or type of food and include at least 3 key facts about your chosen restaurant/food. Where did it originate? How popular is it?

www.cherwell.org

Pizza: the food of globalisation and modern popular culture

By Ferdinand Orleans-Lindsay

Origins of pizza

Pizza is reputed to have been invented in Italy and received its first burst of publicity, when the Neapolitan baker, Rafael Esposito, created a pizza in honour of the Queen of Italy's visit to Naples in 1889. The Queen was Margherita, and the pizza named after her, the Margherita, comprising of the base, tomato sauce and mozzarella, is the most popular pizza of all time.

Essentially, pizza is a savoury dish of Italian origin, consisting, usually, of a round, flattened base of leavened wheat-based dough, topped with tomato sauce, cheese and a variety of other ingredients according to taste, baked at a high temperature, traditionally in a wood-fired oven. It is instructive to note that since its humble beginnings the variety of extra toppings that have made their way on to pizzas has exploded exponentially according to region and taste.

In common with most 'world' foods, pizza has made it across to nearly every corner of the world. It is now not uncommon to visit cities such as Lagos, Accra or Nairobi, to find billboards proclaiming the joys of pizza in colourful headlines. A whole youth culture has now evolved in the 'hip' parts of these burgeoning cities, around going out for a pizza!

The popularity and world domination were assured in part because of the sheer number of Italian immigrants that descended on America (both North and South) between 1880 and 1920. Estimates put the number of Italian immigrants during the period at about 40 million. They brought their taste buds and pizza making expertise with them and the rest, in the well-worn cliché, is history.

Palermo, Italy – the pizza paradise

Today, the Italian city of Palermo, is considered the pizza paradise of the world with the biggest attraction being the 'sfincione' or Sicilian, with its thick crust, heavy splash of local tomato sauce and oodles of melty cheese. The town of Old Forge, Scranton, in the US state of Pennsylvania, however, claims to be the pizza capital of the world. Whatever the validity of these claims, there is no question that pizza has metamorphosed from its humble origins as an experimental Neapolitan delicacy, to the world-beating phenomenon it is today.

Across Europe, in city after city, pizza restaurants have become staples of the high street and it is unthinkable that you will find a major high street anywhere without one. The story is the same across the Atlantic to the United States and Canada, and not even the Chinese and Japanese, with their own well-developed food cultures, have escaped the pizza onslaught.

The ubiquity of pizza

To cement its ubiquity across the globe, the pizza delivery phenomenon, turbo-charged by digital technology across the world, now ensures that any pizza ordered can be delivered to your doorstep in minutes. Such ease of availability ensures that, whether it's for a lazy day in after work, or to celebrate an occasion with family and friends, food can be delivered with little fuss and at such short notice, that a major logistical headache disappears in any such situation where one needs to consider food for the occasion.

Thus have entrepreneurs, seeking to capitalise on the opportunities unearthed, come up with business models that have produced multinational companies based entirely on providing pizza of various sizes, texture and an increasingly bewildering variety of ingredients, to eager customers across the globe. Dominos, Pizza Hut and several other outfits, have become household names, servicing the demand for pizza worldwide.

An amusing feature discovered in pondering the entrails of pizza is that the most unpopular topping are anchovies. Why it continues to be offered is a mystery, but then, there it is. It would appear that the most popular pizzas, judging from the sales figures, are the deep crust version, which is also a mystery to me, as the thin crust variety seems to me to offer superior taste experience. Perhaps, of course, it is a matter of taste.

Pizza as an icon of global culture

Pizza, as the world knows it, first emerged as a veritable part of Italian culture that was exported to the USA with the migration of Italians to the USA in the late 19th century and then to France and then the rest of the world. Today the USA and France are number one and number two respectively in terms of pizza consumption and are thus ahead of the Italians themselves.

The real explosion in the international appeal and popularity of pizza however was to come much later during the early 1960s. As a quick, fast and efficient 'convenience' meal, pizza quickly became a quintessential part of the American way of life. This was the beginning of the internationalisation or even globalisation of pizza as a part of modern popular culture. This was so much so that the Italians sought to reclaim it as part of their culture.

In 2008 the EU granted the Speciality Guaranteed Label to Neapolitan pizza based on features such as the colour, and consistency, rising of the dough to the wood fire cooking as a 'fruit of the creativity of the Neapolitan people'. In 2017 Neapolitan pizza 'twirling' – or the art of the pizza maker – was included on the UNESCO Intangible Cultural heritage List.

Although pizza originated in Italy it found its international success as an expression of cultural hybridity outside its Italian home. A veritable cultural hybrid of globalisation and the modern world, the basic theme with variations of a bread dough base and a smorgasbord of toppings have enabled it to embrace virtually all cultures and identities in the modern world today without it losing the essence of its identity. Everywhere in this world pizza is seen as several things all rolled into one: an exotic food , a street snack and a social meal for sharing with others and very much part of the local culture nearly everywhere in the world today.

We look at the global culture of pizza in a few countries below .

Japan

The usual pizzas found in America and the rest of the world are widely available in Japan, but in addition the Japanese

have their favourite comfort food called okonomiyaki. It is a kind of pizza or savoury pancake. It is made from batter and cabbage and is pan-fried. The toppings are usually selected from a wide variety of toppings such as octopus, shrimp, pork, yam or kimchi.

The dish is popular all over Japan but is particularly associated with the cities of Osaka and Hiroshima.

People in Japan usually eat okonomiyaki in restaurants that specialise in it. The dining tables in such restaurants are usually equipped with an iron griddle called a 'teppan' and customers are given the various ingredients in order to cook the meal themselves. In other restaurants, a chef may do all the cooking to order by customers.

Argentina

Argentina received more migrants from Italy during the 19th and 20th centuries than from any other country. Although Spanish is the official language, the Italian cultural imprint on Argentina is in many ways stronger than the Spanish, especially in and around the country's capital of Buenos Aires.

It therefore stands to reason that pizza in all its glory, shapes, sizes and flavours and toppings would be a big deal in Argentina.

The Argentinian capital Buenos Aires is widely considered to be one of the great pizza capitals of the world. There is a pizza joint on nearly every major city block or at least a small restaurant or food shop that serves pizza among other local offerings such as empanadas, breaded patties and pastas.

The BBC in 2011 reported that there has been a cultural shift in Argentina and the country's favourite traditional meal of the steak was losing pride of place to the pizza. The typical Argentine pizza has a thicker crust than its forebear and counterpart the Italian pizza and usually has a lot more cheese. The most popular toppings for Argentine pizza include anchovies, red peppers, eggs, blue cheese, artichoke hearts and onions. The classic American pizza topping, pepperoni, is hardly served in Argentine pizzeria.

In and around Buenos Aires a popular variation on the general theme of pizza is the fugazetta, which includes a very soft cheese inside the crust mixed with caramelised onions and occasionally ham. A fugazetta is often eaten accompanied by a flatbread made from chickpea flour called a faina. This is made from chickpea flour, water, olive oil and salt and pepper for seasoning.

United Kingdom

Most high streets in the UK have a variety of American and Italian pizza chains as well as local British chains such as Pizza Express, Prezzo and Strada. There are also quite a lot of small independent Italian-run restaurants which serve pizza prepared in wood-fired ovens.

Some of the more exotic toppings popular in the UK include curry toppings such as chicken tikka masala, Italian-American combinations such as Hawaiian (ham and pineapple), pepperoni (spicy salami), meat feast (a mix of meats and salami) and various vegetarian options.

Mushroom pizza has often been voted the most popular in the UK in surveys.

Indonesia

Popular American global pPizza chains like Domino's Pizza and Pizza Hut have a presence in Indonesia.

Although these are all western brands, there are also local pizza brands which offer Indonesian favourite toppings such as satay, rendang and balado. Satay is a an Indonesian or Malaysian dish of seasoned skewered and grilled meat, served with a soy and peanut butter sauce.

Rendang is a local Indonesian spicy red meat dish of which the main ingredients include, meat, coconut milk, chilli, ginger, galangal, turmeric, lemongrass, garlic and shallot.

Balado sauce is made by stir-frying ground red hot chilli pepper with other spices and seasonings such as garlic, shallot, tomato and lime juice in coconut oil or palm oil.

South Korea

Pizza is very popular in South Korea and the global American brands such as Domino's, Pizza Hut and Papa Jon's Pizza compete against local Korean brands such as Mr. Pizza and Pizza Etang.

Pizza is served often with some toppings which are non-traditional idiosyncratically Korean such as corn, potato wedges, sweet potato, shrimp or crab.

Norway

Pizza is extremely popular in Norway and Norwegians, according to some surveys are among the highest consumers of pizza in the world. The most popular by far is what has come to be known in Norway as the frozen pizza brand Grandiosa which some say has become something of a national dish in Norway.

Sweden

Pizzas became popular in Sweden during the 1970s and the arrival of immigrants from Turkey and other Middle Eastern countries has contributed to Swedish pizzas having a discernibly Mediterranean feel and flavour with a dazzling array of different toppings.

Mexico

Mexican-style pizza typically has toppings made from popular Mexican ingredients such as Jalapeño pepper, shrimp, avocado, mozzarella cheese, and chorizo.

Australia

Australian pizza usually has very rich and quintessentially Australian toppings such as chicken, ham, bacon, egg and seafood options such as prawns. There are also quite a few Turkish or Lebanese style kebab shops that sell Middle-eastern style kebabs.

Special sauce to sriracha, globalisation is thriving and terribly broken

By Jeff Israely

For some, it is the most memorable Hollywood dialogue of the late 20th century. Two hitmen driving through Los Angeles (on the way to their next job) are discussing what one calls the 'little differences' between the U.S. and Europe after his visit to Amsterdam and Paris.

You know what they call a Quarter-Pounder with cheese in Paris?

They don't call it a Quarter-Pounder with cheese?

No, they got the metric system there, they wouldn't know what the f*ck a Quarter-Pounder is.

Then what do they call it?

They call it a Royale with cheese

Royale with cheese [smiles]. What do they call a Big Mac?

Big Mac's a Big Mac, but they call it Le Big Mac.

Le Big Mac. [laughs] What do they call a Whopper?

I don't know. I didn't go to Burger King.

The exchange in Quentin Tarantino's Pulp Fiction gives us a singular je-ne-sais-quoi cool from John Travolta and Samuel L. Jackson, as genuine curiosity in that which is foreign meets the utterly mundane.

The movie came out in 1994, at a moment when some believed the Pax Americana was bound to last forever as the Cold War had given way to the global dominance of U.S. culture, commerce … and fast food chains. The opening in 1990 of the first McDonald's in Moscow was hailed as bonafide geopolitical history: The Iron Curtain had come down and the special sauce was flowing.

The same Golden Arches metaphor has been hauled back out in recent weeks – in the inverse – by commentators and politicians alike, as McDonald's closed up all its Russia-based restaurants last month, in response to Vladimir Putin's invasion of Ukraine.

Putin has insisted on a knock-off Russian burger brand taking over the shuttered McDonald's locations, with stories shared about the similar menu, subbing in a new logo and customers barely noticing the difference in the products. Had the Kremlin gotten hold of the secret sauce recipe?

For the Russian president, the rebranded burgers would be proof on the domestic front (as pumped-up energy sales in Asia were abroad) that Moscow could withstand any economic sanctions the West had to present.

As with many other aspects of the Russian war in Ukraine, it is an odd twist to events: counterfeiting American fast food as evidence of standing up to the power of the American economy.

But it's also worth remembering that around the same time that Tarantino's hitmen were pondering the Royale with cheese, celebrated *New York Times* columnist Thomas Friedman had proposed what he called the 'Golden Arches Theory of Conflict Prevention.' As global capitalism expanded, he explained, conflict would eventually dissipate because countries had too much to lose in their economic and commercial relationships. 'No two countries that both have a McDonald's have ever fought a war against each other,' Friedman declared.

Of course, the theory has long since been proven far too optimistic – and as one commentator put it, 'lazy' at its origin.

I have neither the foresight nor energy myself to come up with an alternative. Still, we know that food always gives us something to chew on. The war in Ukraine has set off economic disaster that extends well beyond Russia or McDonald's, and we're currently seeing factors from climate change to blockades to supply chain breakdowns combine to create serious food shortages – risking famine in some places, and elsewhere leaving shoppers without some of their favourite staple goods and consumer products.

That brings us to Sriracha, Thailand's own brand of (spicy) special sauce, which by now is a beloved condiment for a variety of foods around the world. In recent months, a series of circumstances, including drought in Mexico, have caused a shortage of the chili peppers needed to produce Sriracha, and the global supply is expected to remain severely limited for months to come.

It's a missing squirt of spice in the lives of diners around a world where globalized cuisine has long since spread well beyond multilingual McDonald's. It no doubt has the makings of a new theory on where our messy world is heading. Hmmm…?

In the meantime, you know what they call it in Paris: La Sriracha.

25 June 2022

How many McDonald's locations are there in the world?

By Benjamin Elisha Sawe

McDonald's was founded in 1940 by brothers Richard and Maurice McDonald. It was originally intended to be a barbecue restaurant. At present, McDonald's is the second largest chain of fast food restaurants in the world, only after the casual sandwich chain Subway. It has an estimated 36,889 outlets across 120 countries. Around 68 million consumers are served a daily basis. The global headquarters of McDonald's are based in Oak Brook, Illinois, but there is a confirmation that it will be moved to Chicago in early 2018.

Countries with most McD restaurants

McDonald's predominantly sells hamburgers, although its menu varies widely depending on location. In many places, the company has expanded its menu to include salads, fruits, wraps, fish, and smoothies. A McDonald's fast food chain can be run either by an affiliate, the McDonald's Corporation or a franchise. According to a 2012 report published by BBC, McDonald's is the second largest private employer after Walmart accounting for 1.5 million employees.

The history of McDonald's

McDonald's started as a business in 1940 when the McDonald brothers open a small burger joint in San Bernardino, California. At the time, the concept of fast-food was not widespread in American society, although elements had been introduced by early chains such as White Castle. In 1953, the iconic McDonald's golden arches made their debut at a restaurant in Phoenix, Arizona. In 1965 a new clown-like mascot known as Ronald McDonald was introduced in an early example of advertising aimed directly at children.

In 1955 Ray Kroc joined the McDonald's company as a franchise agent, subsequently purchasing the restaurant chain from the two brothers. As Kroc was known for his aggressive business politics, he purchased the McDonald equity from brothers, eventually compelling them to retire from the fast-food business. The company was listed on the public stock market promoting its expansion worldwide. Decades later, it has become a true representation of globalisation.

The top three countries

Since opening in California in the 1950s, McDonald's has expanded considerably throughout the world. At present, McDonald's operates 36,899 restaurants, 5,669 of which are company-owned and 31,230 of which are franchised. Its total property owned is said to have a value between 16 and 18 billion dollars.

United States: The United States is the leading country with the most McDonald's restaurants at 14,145. Approximately 31.5% of revenue collected from the McDonald's Corporation comes from the United States. Most of the McDonald's outlets are concentrated in states that have highest number of people such as California, New York, and Texas. However, the states with the highest number of McDonald's restaurants include Kansas, Louisiana, Ohio, Maryland, and Michigan.

Japan: Japan was the first marketplace for McDonald's in Asia. Japan has about 2,975 outlets although the numbers are said to be reducing considerably.

Countries with the most McDonald's restaurants

Rank	Location	Number of McDonald's
1	United States	14,146
2	Japan	2,975
3	China	2,391
4	Germany	1,470
5	Canada	1,450
6	France	1,419
7	United Kingdom	1,274
8	Australia	920
9	Brazil	812
10	Russia	609
11	Italy	609
12	Spain	497
13	South Korea	450
14	Philippines	449
15	Taiwan	413
16	Mexico	402
17	Poland	400
18	Malaysia	314
19	India	290
20	Turkey	255
21	Netherlands	245
22	Thailand	240
23	Hong Kong	237
24	Sweden	225
25	South Africa	225

Source: WorldAtlas
Note: This information was correct at the time that the article was published, figures will have changed since then.

China: China has the third most McDonald's locations with 2,200 outlets. Despite the franchise having reached Japan and Hong Kong in the 1970s it was not until 1990 when China finally opened the doors to McDonald's. Other leading countries by number of McDonald's restaurants include Germany, France, Canada, and the United Kingdom all of whom have more than 1,000 outlets.

Countries with no McDonald's restaurants

Bermuda does not have any McDonald's due to a government ban on foreign restaurants. Bolivia currently has no McDonald's restaurant, after low sales forced its departure. McDonald's is absent from many countries across Africa, as well as Central Asia.

A symbol of globalisation

McDonald's has become an emblem of globalisation, so much that the term 'McDonaldization' has emerged. *The Economist* magazine uses the Big Mac Index, which compares the Big Mac's cost in different world currencies, which can be used to establish the purchasing power parity (PPP) of currencies. As of July 2015, Switzerland had the world's most expensive Big Mac, while the least expensive is in India followed by Hong Kong.

20 November 2019

Is globalisation leading to a homogenised global culture?

By Rawsab Said

As global connections continue to develop in the twenty-first century under the conditions of globalisation, periphery and semi-periphery nations try to adapt to the norms of core countries with the aim of developing a similar global influence as developed nations. Throughout history, people of different cultures have migrated to countries with cultures different from theirs. As people move from location to location, they bring along their traditions and cultural norms, which influences others to assimilate various aspects of the foreign culture and integrate it into their own. This process is known as cultural diffusion. The spreading of culture can be classified into two categories, forced integration of culture – known as cultural imperialism – and naturally occurring homogenisation. Cultural imperialism is usually due to the colonization or occupation of a country by a foreign power with more global influence.

As the world becomes increasingly globalized, periphery and semi-periphery countries endeavour to reach the same economic positions of core countries, which they undertake by concurring with the cultural norms of highly developed countries. Core countries are tremendously influential, so much so that people that migrate to core countries from lesser developed countries usually acculturate to the cultural standards of the core nation. These give rise to two critical questions of our time: How does homogenisation and hybridisation result from globalisation? What are the pros and cons?

The path to a homogenised global culture?

Core countries, which are nations that are highly developed, can be found at the top of the hierarchy of globally influential countries. This is because these countries are usually industrialized and have periphery and semi-

periphery countries that depend on them. Behind the system of interdependence is a well-functioning, stable, and successful economy, which allows these core countries to be more opulent than others. Being a core country is the primary economic goal of periphery and semi-periphery countries, which is why they often try and follow in the footsteps of developed core nations. The lesser developed countries try to develop themselves in a similar manner to the development of core countries by imitating their culture. This is apparent in many non-core, developing countries. As the world becomes more globalized, all cultures are slowly – but surely – becoming the same. Here, we will use the examples such as the case of Azerbaijan, a developing nation, to show how homogenisation and hybridisation are resulting from globalisation today.

Language

As the number of global connections increase, the need for efficient communication does too. Language serves as both a means and a barrier of interpersonal transmission, which is why the number of international languages has been decreasing for centuries. Many languages spoken exclusively by minorities are dying because the speakers are adapting to more popular languages. In Azerbaijan, the people – especially the youth – are starting to learn English to embrace the culture of developed countries. They also tend to combine some aspects of the Russian language with their own Azerbaijani dialect, which shows the effect and influence of their past occupiers. This expresses the concept of cultural hybridisation, as two cultures are put together instead of one overpowering the other. Another example would be Morocco, in which the people speak a dialect that is a mix of Arabic and French. As for a language that is dying, the Chamicuro language, spoken by the indigenous Chamicuro people of Peru, has become an endangered dialect since the indigenous tribe had decided to become modernized and started to embrace Spanish as their primary language. The transitions of countries to international languages – such as English, French or Arabic – allows for homogenisation as different cultures use the same language, since it makes them become more similar to each other. The uniqueness of cultures is fading as international languages become more common, people are able to communicate with others more easily and more effectively than before. Although many cultures are nearing extinction, many people from different parts of the world are taking the initiative to revive certain languages by learning about them, which is made possible by globalisation, as it allows people to learn more about extinct and endangered languages from around the globe. Languages which are – to some degree – significant to the people that they belong to and their historical context are becoming endangered. For example, Chamicuro, spoken by the Chamicuro tribe in Peru, is becoming replaced with Spanish. This trend can be observed within many tribal languages. This gives a partial representation of the effect of cultural homogenisation, as languages that are widespread are staring to diminish, with international languages replacing them.

Ideologies

In the globalized world that we live in, most of the core countries are secular, which denotes that they are less or not involved in religious or spiritual matters. Many developing countries that attempt to imitate the cultural normalities of developed countries often assimilate secularism in order to create stronger alliances with core countries, as well as to follow the path of progression that was taken by the core countries. Azerbaijan is currently listed as a secular country, which would seem rather unlikely as the majority of the population are Shi'ite Muslim, which tend to be religiously conservative. Cultural hybridisation is also prevalent in this example, since Azerbaijan is an openly progressive country, but at the same time it retains its unitary government. This exemplifies the notion that core countries influence developing countries through means such as political doctrines. Other political ideologies include democracies and progressivism. Since different countries with significantly different cultures have the same ideologies, which dictate their values and make them increasingly similar. This is more of an advantage, as countries with parallel beliefs and ideologies have a tendency to develop stronger alliances. Although countries having similar ideologies provides several benefits, it still offers a few disadvantages, for example, some countries choose to have different political dogmas because of its culture, majority religion, or geographic location, which causes uncertainty of the relationship with countries that have differing ideologies. A country's ideologies – whether it be political or social – are substantially important to how it is viewed, which impacts its global influence.

Cultural arts

Cultural arts are a major part of a country's unique norms and traditions, especially in lesser-developed countries where folk music and art are more prevalent than modernist values of highly developed countries. Azerbaijan used to be known for its Mugham – a folk musical composition that was regarded as a highly complex art form that fused together classic poetry and musical improvisation – but now it is known for its operas and plays that take place in its theatres. Originally, opera was an Italian art which was embraced by many nations that are now core countries. Since Azerbaijan is one of the countries that imitates the culture of developed countries, it includes opera as one of its cultural art forms, which conveys the country's homogenisation of particularly

'Western' culture. Traces of cultural imperialism can also be found in the roots of Azerbaijani culture as some remnants of Russian culture can be found in the country's art, which was due to the forced Russian occupation of Azerbaijan. Cultural homogenisation is prevalent, as different cultures assimilate art forms of other cultures which cause them to become even more similar than they were before. On the other hand, through increased global connections, people can also have the opportunity to learn about foreign cultural arts and study them, which allows them to be preserved and not forgotten. Cultural arts are undeniably a preeminent facet of individual cultures that reflect the distinctive values that people believe in, so the assimilation towards similar, if not the same, art forms can diminish the concept of personal identity. On the other hand, progressing towards a single form of art would allow both core and periphery countries to better relate to one another, thus developing stronger bonds between nations.

Other forms of influence

Globalisation is a means of influence for core countries, since developing countries with the aim to improve economically look up to developed countries and follow in their footsteps. Cultural homogenisation – as well as hybridisation – takes place, since the cultures of periphery and semi-periphery countries are susceptible to changes, as adaptations towards cultures of developed countries gives people a sense of improvement, since they are able to relate to more developed countries and follow the same progressive pattern as core nations. Apart from language, ideologies, and cultural arts, cultural homogenisation is prevalent through architecture, food, and fashion. As the world progresses, so does architecture. Newer building designs are innovated to accommodate the growing population and modernism that resides in developed countries, which are reproduced by influenced periphery and semi-periphery countries. In non-core countries, ultra-modern architecture shows the substantial influence that core countries have. Modern architecture abolishes cultural identity in cities, but at the same time it allows for more stable architecture and accommodation for growing populations. Although new, modern architecture is being developed, Azerbaijan still has some towns which retain traditional Turkish-Azerbaijani houses and buildings. There are a few foreign designer clothing brands, such as Gucci and Balenciaga that are pinpointed in the city of Baku, Azerbaijan, which shows the influence of more developed countries through terms of fashion. This doesn't serve any significant advantages, other than lessening discrimination and security concerns caused by foreign clothing. The influence of modern clothing choice and popular 'fashion' demolishes the concept of individualism through cultural clothing. On the contrary, many Azerbaijanis retain some cultural aspects through religion, as many Muslim women wear the headscarf for religious – and cultural – purposes. Foreign fast food restaurants, such as McDonald's and KFC, are also prevalent in non-core countries such as Azerbaijan. Foreign fast food restaurants allow more job opportunities for people in developing countries, but it also diminishes the cultural taste preferences of the local people. But some fast food companies change certain menu items to fit in with the cultural food of the country that their restaurants are in, which allows for cultural hybridisation

through means of 'glocalisation'. Although the number of fast-food restaurants is increasing, Azerbaijani households usually serve the same traditional food, as it relies on the readily available ingredients distinctive to Azerbaijan. There are many other forms of influence from core countries that affect the cultures of periphery and semi-periphery countries, whether it be a positive change that allows for more advantages, or a negative change that causes more disadvantages to the developing country.

Cultures of different countries are slowly becoming more and more similar as global connections and foreign influences increase. At one point, individual cultures may become almost the same as the cultures that influence them, which are mainly the highly developed core countries with the most economic influence. Developing countries aiming to economically progress to the level of core countries try to do so by adapting to the cultural norms of global superpowers. This usually results in homogenisation, where cultures become increasingly similar, so much so that a single global culture has the possibility to be established. Countries that have been occupied or invaded in the past also retain remnants of their invaders' culture, which is known as cultural imperialism. Lastly, some countries try to coalesce their own cultures with the cultures of other nations to adapt to modern 'culture' and retain their own identity simultaneously, which was described as cultural hybridisation. By analysing the examples of Azerbaijan – as well as other developing countries – the progression towards one global culture is prevalent, with the most influential cultural aspects being of developed Western nations. In summary, core countries with great economic control often influence countries with the objective of major development to adapt to their culture, slowly bringing us to a more unified, global culture.

3 November 2021

Does globalisation threaten our cultural identity?

In the world of today, globalisation is often regarded as a threat to the cultural identity of groups or even countries. Let's contemplate on which levels it does and on which it does not.

By Eva Rutten

All societies worldwide have been creating closer connections for centuries, but the speed at which connections are formed has increased due to recent developments in communication and globalisation. International companies have been creating one global market in which flying, telephone services, email, computers, cars and steady incomes have become interdependent of one another. People are affirming and defending their identities and cultures they belong to in the need to be unique. To understand the impact on cultural identity, cultural identity needs to be further illustrated.

Your cultural identity provides the feeling of belonging to a group with similar characteristics. It includes how you see yourself, your nationality, ethnicity, beliefs and religion, social class and if you belong to a group that has his own culture[1]. It is the way of life through which you define yourself and add value to your social relationships[2]. A culture is not something that stands still, it changes and grows. Culture does not necessarily change in relation to economic and political circumstances. It changes and alters in dialogue with other cultures which they come across with through economic and political relations. Because people create cultures themselves, the alteration of them is subject to whether they reject or integrate other cultural influences[3].

Cultural identity can be evaluated at three levels[4]. The first dimension, humans relate to life by producing goods and selling or exchanging them. The second dimension represents cultural activities to structure their relationships and build communities. The third level is about how they look and motivate themselves to reach goals by following their beliefs and religion. 'These three levels provide an identity to a social group and distinguish it from other groups'[4].

Globalisation is the flows of people, organisations, capital, images and ideas across the globe, let's see what kind of effect this has on these 3 dimensions.

First Dimension: The economy

The first dimension will look at the economy. Multinational companies are producing and selling products to customers all over the world nowadays. Advocates against the principle

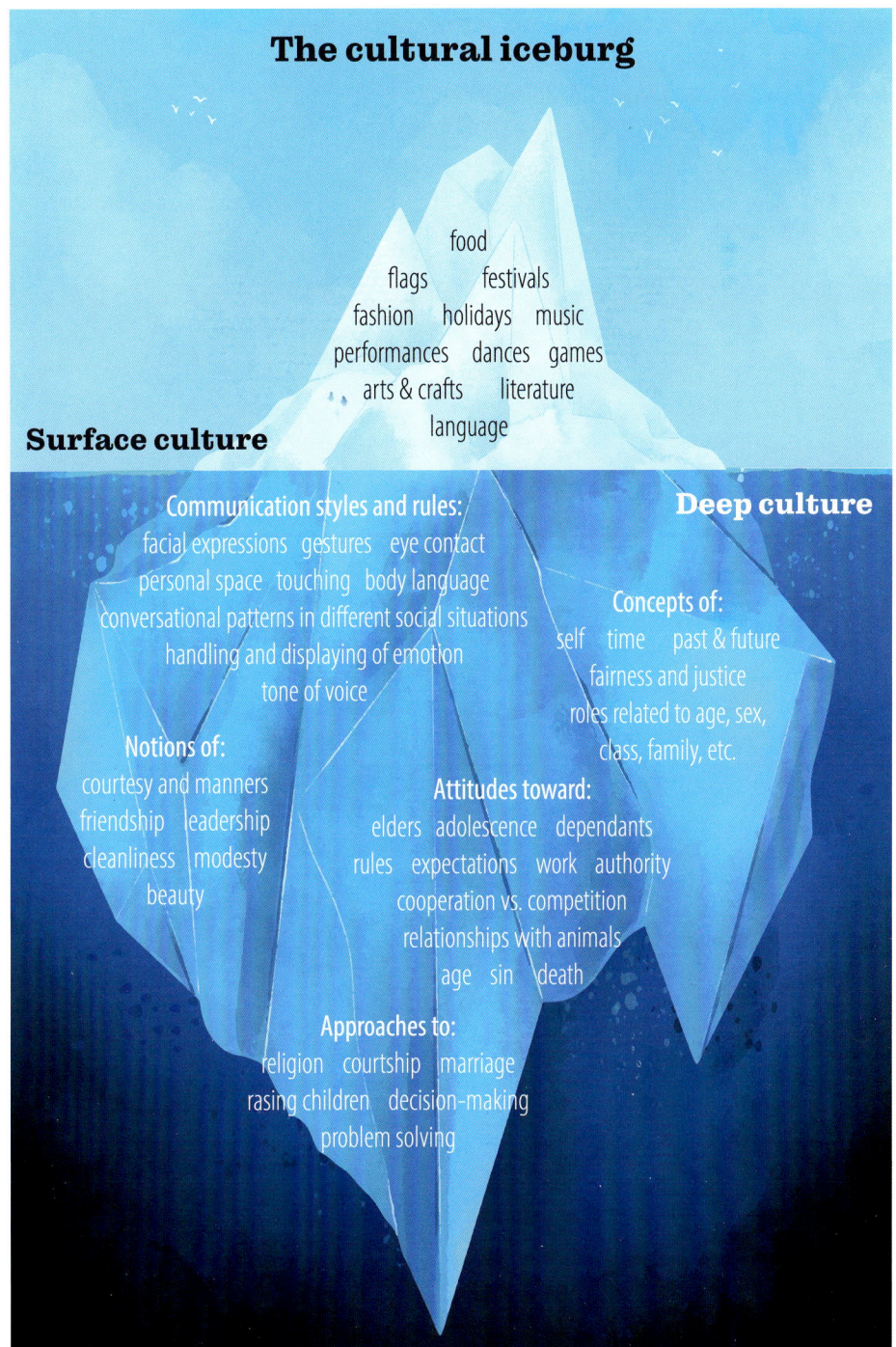

The cultural iceburg

Surface culture

food
flags   festivals
fashion   holidays   music
performances   dances   games
arts & crafts   literature
language

Deep culture

Communication styles and rules:
facial expressions   gestures   eye contact
personal space   touching   body language
conversational patterns in different social situations
handling and displaying of emotion
tone of voice

Concepts of:
self   time   past & future
fairness and justice
roles related to age, sex,
class, family, etc.

Notions of:
courtesy and manners
friendship   leadership
cleanliness   modesty
beauty

Attitudes toward:
elders   adolescence   dependants
rules   expectations   work   authority
cooperation vs. competition
relationships with animals
age   sin   death

Approaches to:
religion   courtship   marriage
rasing children   decision-making
problem solving

of globalisation claim that countries are being homogenised into a new global area, in which consumer goods are all the same. 'With this goes a consumeristic way of life and system of values that concentrate on the material world and on physical comfort'[5]. In this way you could say that cultural characteristics are lost, and identities are eliminated.

However, even though goods are being homogenised, people can still differentiate themselves by having great freedom in selecting what they want to buy. They can choose what they want regardless of what is passed on to them and product and service development are tailored to more and more ethnic and cultural preferences. This global development cannot decrease culture diversity because all people have the right to choose what they believe in, what to buy, and how to represents their own cultural identity.

Second Dimension: Cultural activities and social relationships

The second dimension talks about cultural activities and social relationships. It is said that business cultures can also be harmonised to become more and more the same. But, these do not affect how they structure their personal relationships and build relationships with people close to them. Relationships are not limited because of homogenisation[3].

If you look at schools like the Skyline University College, you will see that just like AMSIB they created a multicultural environment in which over 30 nationalities live alongside each other. Despite the differences in values, culture, and language we won't change or abandon who we are just because we come across something different. We learn to live and grow with each other to improve performance and include the diversity[6] [7]. Inclusion in combination with diversity can actually lead to greater individual benefits and corporate improvement, such as, productivity, innovation, and financial gain[6].

Third Dimension: Beliefs and religion

Moving to the third dimension. According to Zygmunt Bauman, who wrote about the human consequences of globalisation, 'Sociologists have frequently pointed out that while religion loses its dominant position and modernity has led to a differentiation of social institutions, modernity has not managed to become a substitute for religions for most people'[8]. Globalisation can provide opportunities to learn and explore cultural differences across the world. And it also works the other way around, it can give you the chance to represent your culture and give others the chance to explore yours. Cultures are imbedded values of groups of people that cannot suddenly disappear. Globalisation helps improve our awareness of different societies by not forgetting our own.

In these above-mentioned views globalisation has minimal effect, but globalisation does have effect on smaller cultures that are not common and have not enough critical mass to continue existing. For those cultural identities' globalisation poses a threat. But it has also affected more developed countries. In Japan, industrialisation and technology has led to declining traditions in their culture, such as, arts, social practices, and artisanship)[9]. But because of it they benefited from the growth of democracy and poverty reduction. And so on, globalisation can eliminate cultural societies and in return could alter and recreate new identities. People will always adapt and find new cultural identities to belong to.

Other studies discovered that many languages are on the verge of being extinct due to the development of globalisation. There are around 7000 spoken languages in the world. Around 71% of those spoken are estimated to be in danger in a few years and half of those are even losing their value in the world because they are not used for any purpose. Languages are under threat when under 1000 people are able to speak it[10].

Final thoughts

To conclude, globalisation can have a positive and negative impact on individual identities and those of groups and countries. All these factors show that the effects of globalisation do not change how people find meaning in life, they can identify themselves by deciding what to buy, where they buy and how it represents them. It also does not take away the freedom of choosing where to belong as an individual and as a group. Beliefs and social relationships can be structured without the effect of global influence but can also grow and improve because of it. On the downside, the impact of globalisation on cultural heritage and languages can be considered a threat when the culture exists below a critical mass of 1000 this would mean they would slowly disappear and become extinct.

Take a look at the picture on the previous page. In what way do you think globalisation can lead to a loss or gain of cultural identity?

28 March 2021

Here's what a Korean boy band can teach us about globalisation 4.0

By Peter Vanham, Deputy Head of Media, World Economic Forum Geneva

For the readers of America's *TIME* Magazine, it was clear: Korean boy band BTS should be 2018 Person of the Year. After a worldwide online poll, they held onto their early lead to beat candidates like Planet Earth and US President Donald Trump.

But who is BTS? Well, unless you've been living under a rock this past year (like me), you wouldn't ask that question. The K-pop sensation scored two number one albums in the Billboard Top 200, beat Justin Bieber to become Top Social Artist of 2018, and are the most talked about artists in the world.

In their global success, though, one peculiarity stands out. Their songs are mostly sung in Korean, not English. They are not alone in this phenomenon. Latin artists like Fonsi (Despacito) and Enrique Iglesias, or fellow Korean artists like Psy (Gangnam Style), are showing that the globalisation of culture no longer only coincides with Americanisation. Will we see a more diverse globalisation as of now?

From the end of World War Two to the 2000s, the arrow of cultural globalisation pointed in only one direction: that of the English language and American culture.

Whereas many European countries until the 1960s were still most influenced by French culture, the tide had started to shift from 1945. American GIs had come to Europe to fight, but they also brought Coca-Cola, jazz music and an admiration of Hollywood films. On other continents too, the rising economic and political power of America translated into a rising cultural influence.

Indeed, as many Asian and European societies were focused on rebuilding, American culture conquered the world. Elvis Presley, Frank Sinatra, Marvin Gaye, Aretha Franklin and James Brown started the trend. As the decades went by, only Brits and other English language artists like The Beatles and the Rolling Stones could really keep pace with their American peers.

Today, there is no denying the dominant global culture is American. The highest grossing films of all time, worldwide, are almost without exception from Hollywood (think Avatar, Titanic or Star Wars). The best-selling albums of all time are mostly American (although Australian band AC/DC and British band Pink Floyd gave Michael Jackson a run for his money).

Most social-media and internet firms are American. And food culture, though more diverse, is still affected by the McDonald's, Coca-Cola's, Starbucks and PepsiCo's of this world.

The world's most spoken languages

Estimated number of first-language speakers worldwide in 2017 (millions)*

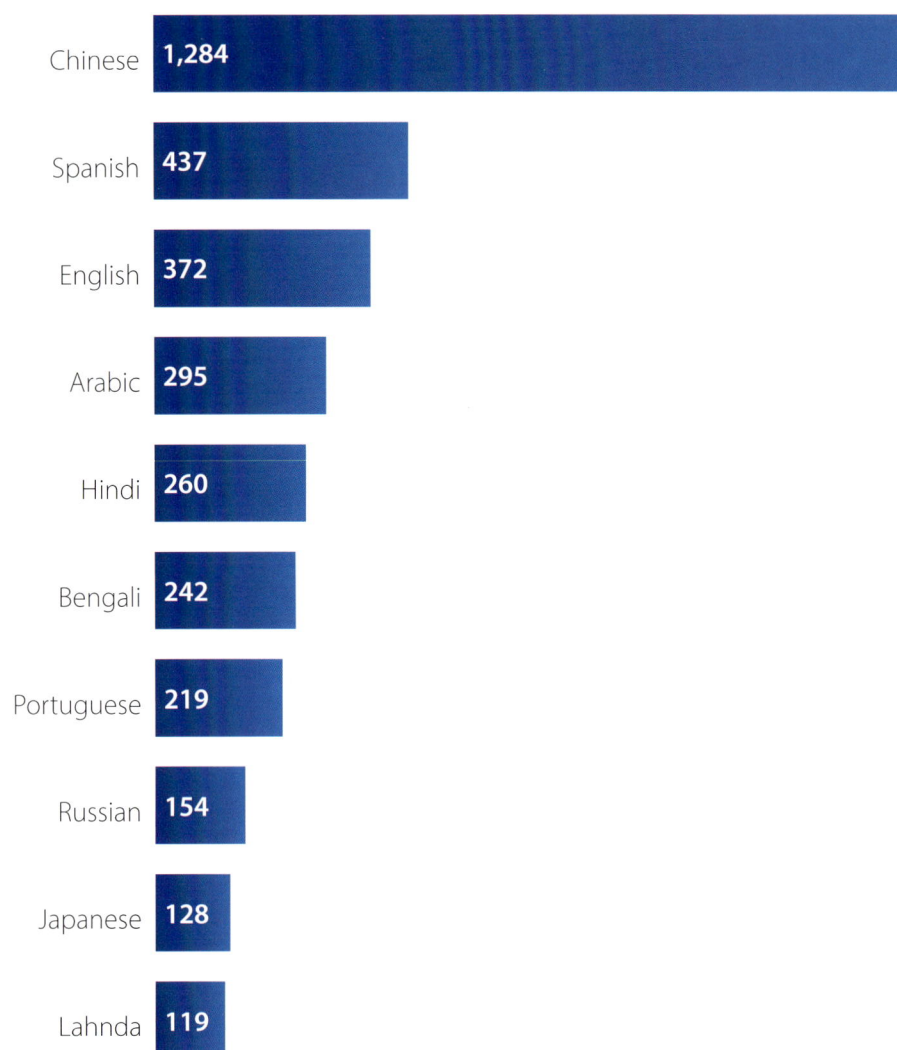

Language	Speakers (millions)
Chinese	1,284
Spanish	437
English	372
Arabic	295
Hindi	260
Bengali	242
Portuguese	219
Russian	154
Japanese	128
Lahnda	119

*Each language also includes associated member langauges and varieties
Source: Ethnologue

This evolution would not have been possible without the wider globalisation of the world economy, and the transformative impact of technology. In the 1960s, transatlantic flights and radio recordings made it possible for The Beatles to unleash a mania in America. In the 1990s and 2000s open global markets and the internet allowed for cultural sensations to spread even faster.

The dark side of globalised culture

But this globalisation of culture did come at a price. Consider languages. Since the earliest era of globalisation – the 16th Century Age of Discovery – the number of spoken languages worldwide has steadily declined, from about 14,500 to less than 7,000.

By 2007, the New York Times reported, half of the remaining 7,000 languages were at danger of extinction. And by 2017, the World Economic Forum wrote, almost 1,500 languages had less than 1,000 speakers left.

As UNESCO, the United Nations' educational, scientific and cultural arm pointed out at Rio+20, the homogenisation of culture brought other risks too.

It said in 2012: 'While this phenomenon promotes the integration of societies, it may also bring with it a loss of uniqueness of local culture, which in turn can lead to loss of identity, exclusion and even conflict.' Recent outbursts of violence incited through global social media like Facebook and Twitter show it was a prescient view.

Then there are the economic effects of a globalising culture. Already before the rise of social media and the so-called Big Tech companies, less than a dozen companies – like Disney, 21st Century Fox, Sony and Viacom – owned the lion's share of the world's leading media and entertainment institutions.

The arrival of large tech platforms only accelerated the trend towards larger market concentration, and the risks of loss of cultural diversity.

Finally, as much as we may like our burger with fries, our bag of chips and our takeaway cup of coffee, the globalising fast-food culture exacerbated global problems too.

If everyone consumed the same amount of burgers as Americans, or created as much rubbish, climate change and pollution might be insurmountable, and obesity an even bigger cause of illness and death.

Time bomb, or boon?

This raises some important questions. Is American-led cultural globalisation a self-destructive time bomb, destined to slowly kill languages, cultures and life itself? Is cultural globalisation a phenomenon that enriches local cultures with a diverse set of foreign influences? Or should we be agnostic about it, as long as it leads to more positive outcomes for society and the environment, like better governance and climate leadership?

If, until recently, the first question seemed most likely to be answered 'yes', BTS, Fonsi and their peers showed a more diverse globalisation can't be completely written off.

Take the case of Luis Fonsi first. With his hit single Despacito, the Puerto Rican singer broke seven Guinness World Records, including first YouTube video to reach 5 billion views, and most streamed track worldwide. Doing so, he showed that you can influence global culture through the Spanish language and Caribbean culture too. This is unsurprising when you consider that there are 437 million people who speak Spanish as a first language compared to 372 million native English speakers.

The case of BTS is perhaps even more impressive, because it is so much more against the cultural odds. While Spanish, alongside Mandarin Chinese and English belongs to the top 3 of most spoken languages worldwide, Korean doesn't even feature in the top 10. As a matter of fact, Korea until about a century ago was known as the 'Hermit Kingdom', for its cultural and economic isolation.

There are still remnants of Korea's isolation today. In many other G20 economies, like France or Germany, English language songs counted for the majority of hits by 2017. In Korea all top hits were still Korean. BTS is no exception. Most of their songs are largely sung in Korean, with only parts of the lyrics in English. Yet, BTS managed to become the global musical sensation of the year.

What's more, their success is in part bottom-up, with many fans helping the band voluntarily to translate and subtitle their music videos and performances to English. And BTS is also not the first K-pop band to break through internationally. In the West, Psy is well-known, but across Asia, including in China, Vietnam, and Japan, many more K-pop bands are vastly popular.

Of course, one swallow does not a summer make, nor will Fonsi and BTS change cultural globalisation single-handedly. But in other domains too, cultural power players have emerged from elsewhere than America. Asia in particular is rising in cultural influence.

The first AI news anchor, for example, comes from China, and speaks both Mandarin and English. Hollywood is increasingly influenced by and working with Chinese companies and actors, like The Great Wall with Matt Damon and Jing Tian, or one of the hit movies of this year, Crazy Rich Asians, which featured an all-Asian cast, and was based on an equally successful series of books.

In the field of technology, Swedish-based Spotify managed to become one of the most successful streaming companies.

And in the world of sports, both the FIFA World Cup of football, and the Olympic Games pride themselves in celebrating a diverse set of nations and cultures, though they faced criticism for failing to lead on governance.

For all the criticism the leaders of the Americanisation of global culture face, some of its most famous representative companies have also been leading the world in positive cultural change.

The bigger picture

The World Economic Forum's Saadia Zahidi wrote in her book *50 Million Rising* that McDonald's was among the first to integrate women in the workforce in Muslim-majority countries like Indonesia and Saudi-Arabia.

And PepsiCo, under the leadership of its Indian-born CEO Indra Nooyi, has been shifting away from sugary drinks, and investing in businesses like Sodastream, which commercialise carbonised tap water and eliminate plastic.

But those may turn out to be elements that miss the bigger cultural picture of 2018. The fact that singers and bands from the Caribbean and Korea can make the world's most popular music show that there is nothing inevitable about the Americanisation of cultural globalisation after all.

More likely, cultures will continue to exist and cross-fertilize each other, as they have for centuries.

It is important for all to embrace their own culture, and for policymakers and other stakeholders to strengthen and promote cultural bonds in society. But if a boy band from the Hermit Kingdom can become Person of the Year in the economic capital of the world, a global monoculture is still quite a way away.

Madeleine Hillyer contributed to this article.

18 December 2018

Useful Websites

www.cherwell.org

www.concordiajournal.com

www.countercurrents.org

www.economicshelp.org

www.ecoresolution.earth

www.grahamsquires.com

www.imperial.ac.uk

www.theconversation.com

www.weforum.org

www.wired.co.uk

www.worldatlas.com

www.worldcrunch.com

References:

Page 37-38

1. (W. Morris, Mok, & Mor, 2011)
2. (Featherstone, 1996)
3. (Yi Wang, Harbin Engineering University, China, 2007)
4. (Appadurai, 1996)
5. (Featherstone, Lash & Robertson, 1995)
6. (Nguyen-Phuong-Mai, 2019)
7. (Students, 2017)
8. (Bauman, 1998)
9. (Flowers, 2018)
10. (Held & Anthony, 2004)

Affluence

Wealth; abundance of money or valuable resources.

Brexit

An abbreviation that stands for 'British exit'. Referring to the referendum that took place on 23 June 2016 where British citizens voted to exit the European Union. Britain left the EU on 31 January 2020, but a trade deal was finally reached on 24 December 2020.

Capitalism

An economic system in which wealth generation is driven by privately-owned enterprises and individuals, rather than the state.

Community

People living in one particular place or people who are considered a unit due to their shared values, beliefs or identity.

Deglobalisation

The slow-down or reverse of globalisation. Deglobalisation is the process of diminishing interdependence and integration between nations.

Economy

The way in which a region manages its resources. References to the 'national economy' indicate the financial situation of a country: how wealthy or prosperous it is.

Free trade

An economic policy which promotes the free movement of goods and services between countries and the elimination of restrictions to trading between nations, such as import and export tariffs.

Globalisation

Globalisation is a term used to explain the increased social and trade-related exchanges between nations. It implies that nations are moving closer together economically and culturally. In recent years, through the Internet, air travel, trade and popular culture, globalisation has rapidly increased.

Gross Domestic Product (GDP)

The total value of the goods and services produced in a country within a year. This figure is used as a measure of a country's economic performance.

Immigration

To immigrate is to move permanently from your home country, and settle somewhere else.

Inflation

A measure of the rate of rising prices of goods and services in an economy.

International Monetary Fund (IMF)

The International Monetary Fund (IMF) is an international organisation set up to oversee the global financial system and stabilise exchange rates.

Internet

A worldwide system of interlinked computers, all communicating with each other via phone lines, satellite links, wireless networks and cable systems.

Liberalisation

The relaxation of government restrictions such as barriers to free trade.

Migration

To migrate is to move from one's home country and settle in another.

Multiculturalism

A number of different cultures coexisting side-by-side, for example within a school or a country.

Multinational corporations (MNCs)

Powerful companies which operate in more than one country. Due to their size and large economies, multinational corporations – sometimes called transnational corporations (TNCs) – can hold substantial influence over governments and local economies.

NAMA

The World Trade Organization members negotiate on many different areas in order to increase liberalisation. Agriculture and public services (GATS) are two of the more well known areas. Another is called non-agricultural market access (NAMA). These negotiations aim to remove barriers to free trade in all industrial goods and natural resources. For example, NAMA seeks to take down import tariffs, which make imported goods more expensive.

Nationalism

Nationalism is often considered to be more aggressive than patriotism, implying the desire to be a completely separate nation and intolerance of influences from other cultures. For example, a Welsh patriot might feel proud to be Welsh and love their country's culture and values, but still be happy to be a part of the United Kingdom. A Welsh nationalist might feel that Wales should be separate from the UK, and feel intolerant of people or things from outside their country.

Protectionism

The policy of protecting domestic industries from foreign competition by restricting trade between nations.

Recession

A period during which economic activity has slowed, causing a reduction in Gross Domestic Product (GDP), employment, household incomes and business profits. If GDP shows a reduction over at least six months, a country is then said to be in recession. Recessions are caused by people spending

Glossary

less, businesses making less and banks being more reluctant to give people loans.

Sovereign debt

In the 1970s, rich oil-producing countries put their massive profits into banks to earn interest. To pay this interest, the banks made loans to developing countries. Interest rates were low, and these loans were thought to be affordable. It hardly mattered what the loans were used for because the borrowing governments guaranteed the debt. This is called 'sovereign debt'.

Sustainable Development Goals (SDGs)

17 goals set out by the United Nations to protect the planet and ensure that people around the world can live with equality and in a healthy environment by 2030. The goals cover social, economic and environmental sustainability. 'End poverty in all its forms everywhere' is the number one SDG.

Tariff

A tax placed on imported and exported goods.

Trade

When you buy a computer game or a bar of chocolate, you are 'trading': exchanging money for goods. Workers, companies, countries and consumers take part in trade. Workers make or grow the goods. Companies pay the workers and sell what they produce. Governments encourage companies to set up; they create jobs, generate taxes and earn foreign currency. Consumers buy the end product.

World Bank

An organisation set up to reduce poverty by providing loans for developing countries.

World Trade Organization (WTO)

An international organisation first set up in 1995 to monitor the rules of international trade and promote free trade between countries. The WTO has the power to impose fines or sanctions on member countries that do not follow the rules of trade. Critics of the WTO argue that it holds too much power and protects the interests of rich countries to the disadvantage of developing countries.

Index